Crime And Chaos

In Victorian Penkridge

By the same author:

Tales From Four Towns - Death, Destruction, Crime and Notable News from 19th Century Walsall, Wednesbury, West Bromwich and Wolverhampton.

Coven In Times Past

Crime And Chaos

In Victorian Penkridge

Paul Robinson

Penk Publishing

ISBN 978-1-326-34251-7

Penk Publishing

Email: penk.publishing@gmail.com

Contents

Foreword

As the title suggests, the events described in this book took place during the long reign (1837-1901) of Queen Victoria, although I have taken the liberty of including a few stories from the decades either side of her rule.

In most cases, the details are taken from contemporary newspaper accounts and, then as now, errors sometimes found their way into the reports, especially when it came to the spelling of names and places. Where possible, I have checked the details against other records and made the necessary corrections in the text. That said, there may still be mistakes lurking in the original documents as well as errors of my own making.

Sources for the various sections of each chapter are listed at the end of the book, to enable readers to check the details for themselves.

Introduction

As much of this book concerns crime of one sort or another, it is worth briefly considering how the law was applied in practice during the nineteenth century. There was no police force in the modern sense until the 1850s; before this there was an 'area constable' assisted by watchmen, acting under the supervision of a Justice of the Peace appointed by the crown - a system that had been in place since medieval times.

Landowners and farmers also availed themselves of gamekeepers and bailiffs to protect their interests. When public order was threatened, as it sometimes was by rioting miners, Luddites or others with a political grievance, there was little option but to call out the army to protect the peace.

There were essentially three tiers of justice in the Victorian era; Petty Sessions, sometimes referred to as Police Courts, were the forerunners of Magistrates' Courts and dealt with lower level crimes and later, licensing and other such matters. These were held at police stations or local chambers sometimes known as 'justice rooms'.

Matters requiring a higher court were sometimes passed to the Quarter Sessions, so called because they were held quarterly, at

Stafford. The most serious crimes, and occasionally civil matters, were referred to the Assizes and the 'circuit judges'.

Penkridge's Petty Sessions were at one time held at the Littleton Arms, but from the 1880s they were conducted at the police station, housed in what was originally a savings bank but is now the village library. Aside from the court room, the building included quarters for a sergeant, a constable and two prison cells.

The magistrate's court could hand down a custodial sentence or a fine, and the former might also include hard labour at the 'house of correction'. Hard labour would often consist of picking oakum; that is, unravelling the individual fibres from tarred ropes for re-use as caulking. It was extremely hard and dirty work, usually resulting in severely blistered and blackened hands.

Hard labour at a prison might include being made to walk the treadmill. A few such man-powered mills created an end product, flour for example, but most produced nothing and were used solely as a form of punishment. An alternative to the treadmill was the crank, an equally pointless hand operated machine with variable resistance - both were despised by prisoners. Those sentenced to hard labour were also frequently put to the task of stone-breaking or co-opted into road and dock construction.

The gravest offences might result in extended prison terms or ultimately in capital punishment. Transportation for a specified number of years or for life was also common punishment for such felonies, although it was sometimes used for much less serious crimes.

For those down on their luck and with no other means of support, the poor laws and the workhouse provided a buffer against utter destitution. Inmates were segregated by gender and made to work for their keep, unless they were so ill that they were lodged in the infirmary. It was not uncommon for seasonal workers, children of the poor and single mothers to be in and out of the workhouse over several years.

Penkridge had a workhouse in the village in the late eighteenth century, located on the Cannock Road. It usually housed a little over a hundred poor souls and provided 'outdoor relief' to many hundreds of vagrants every month. After the establishment of the Penkridge Poor Law Union in the 1830's, people were sent to the workhouse at Brewood - all bedding and furniture from the old workhouse was sold off at an auction in 1837. In the last quarter of the century, a new building was erected on the Wolverhampton Road at Cannock and the Union was subsequently renamed to reflect its new location.

For those too young to remember our old 'imperial' system of currency, it will help to know that money was specified in pounds, shillings and pence; there were twelve pence to a shilling and twenty shillings to a pound. Shillings and pence are sometimes abbreviated to 's' and 'd' in the text, for example, 7s 6d being seven shillings and six pence (or “seven and six” as people said at the time). Calculating the relative value of money in the past is difficult, but for the century or so covered by this book, £1 was a significant amount of money to the vast majority of the population - wages were often in pence or shillings per week and many items of food and drink cost just a penny or two.

Chapter 1 - Drink & Deceit

One Over The Eight

Although beer in Victorian Britain was somewhat weaker than it is today, many working class men thought that eight pints could be safely consumed before becoming intoxicated. It is unsurprising then, that court reports for almost any week in the nineteenth century show that Penkridge, like virtually every other village and town in the land, was plagued by drunken behaviour.

The offences were usually minor and sometimes have a humorous side when viewed from this distance in time, but occasionally they were associated with more serious offences such as fighting or assaulting police officers. For misdemeanours at the lower end of the scale, the transgressors usually ended up with a fine of a few shillings, with progressively higher tariffs, sometimes including imprisonment, for infractions of a more serious nature.

In addition to the present (and recently closed) pubs, there were several other 'watering holes' in the village during the nineteenth century; the Blacksmith's Arms, The Swan Inn at Swan Lane, the Lord Nelson Inn, The Plough at Pillaton and so on. In the middle years of the century there may also have been one or more beer-houses - private dwellings licensed to sell beer but not spirits.

Given all these options, the 'one over the eight mindset' and the comparatively low price of beer, it is hardly surprising that drunkenness was rife.

A look at a few typical cases from the 1880s shows the order of fines handed down for being drunk and disorderly:

- Joseph Barnes, a blacksmith of Boscomoor was fined 10 shillings, including costs, for being drunk on the Wolverhampton Road on the evening of 18th January 1884.

- Cannock magistrates fined stone-mason, William Berry for being drunk at Penkridge on two separate occasions - eighteen shillings was the total tariff imposed.

- At the petty sessions in May 1888: Henry Weatherer, labourer, drunk and disorderly in Stone Cross, fine and costs of 13 shillings; William Simcox, labourer, drunk and disorderly in Stone Cross, fine and costs of 10 shillings; a number of men from Coven and Huntington faced similar charges and penalties on the same day.

- At the Police Court on Monday 3rd September 1888: Albert Faulkner, bricklayer, drunk and disorderly in Market Street, fine and cost over 21 shillings; William Talbot, labourer, drunk and disorderly on the Cannock Road, fine and costs of 16 shillings.

At least Market Street labourer William Dodd was able to offer us something different - in August 1888 he was fined 6 shillings with

11 shillings and sixpence in costs for being drunk and disorderly. Investigating a disturbance on the street at around 10:20 pm, Sergeant Titterton found Dodd drunk and completely stripped of his clothes!

Being 'under the influence' at work these days is usually a serious disciplinary matter, but in the past employees frequently worked in various states of inebriation. Even in potentially dangerous places like factories, farms and within the transport industry, it was commonplace for workers to visit the pub at lunchtime and return to operate their dangerous machinery with happy abandon during the afternoon. Larger institutions, especially those where public safety might be a concern, were rather more fastidious.

Around the end of the 1800s the Royal Mail offered a phenomenally efficient service, with many letters being delivered on the same day that they were posted. This was only possible when all the cogs in the machine (the post offices, sorters, postmen, mail trains and so on) ran smoothly and without interruption.

In 1890, Daniel Harrison of Hednesford was hauled before the Petty Sessions for being of being drunk in charge of the mail-cart at Penkridge. Harrison was said to be totally incapable of controlling the cart and another driver had to be seconded to take the mail on to Stafford. Harrison's employers took an extremely dim view of the matter and he was fired. As he had lost his job and was also in frail heath, the Bench let him off - on payment of 7 shillings in costs!

Another mail-cart driver was in trouble at Penkridge a few years later although not because of drink: Frederick Allen of Chadsmoor was charged with 'game trespass', that is taking game from land without a licence. In fact it was Allen's dog who did the trespassing, witnessed by a farm labourer at Teddesley Coppice. The dog initially chased a hare but veered off to take a rabbit, which had become entangled in some wire, and carried it back to his master who was waiting down the road beside his cart.

Allen said he always took the dog with him for company but the magistrate said he would have to keep it under control in future - especially as he had caused the same farmer £50 worth of damage during the lambing season. He was handed a £1 fine plus costs.

George Selwyn of Wolverhampton had his coat, gloves and pipe stolen while visiting Penkridge's National School, for entertainment (perhaps a Christmas play or concert) on the evening of 10th December 1899. Mr Selwyn informed the police as soon as the theft was noticed and a little later in the evening Sergeant Campbell arrested a man in the street who was wearing the coat. When asked his name, the drunken man told the officer "you will have to find out", although he later gave his name as James Matthews of no fixed address.

In April 1900, William Price of Levedale didn't have to face his usual long walk home after visiting the pub, he was instead arrested for being drunk and disorderly in Clay Street. Twelve shillings was the total penalty imposed. At the same hearing, some thirty shillings in fines and costs were handed down to Thomas Hadrian a local labourer. He was drunk and using bad language but kicked out at the two officers who came to arrest him. Assaulting the police carried a much stiffer penalty.

In 1901 Alfred Jones, alias Pearson, was fined 1s plus 5s costs for being drunk and disorderly in Stone Cross - he had recently been warned by Sergeant Campbell for similar behaviour. Two years later officer Campbell was still dealing with the same old problem; George Bott of Micklewood was fined a similar amount to Jones.

Charles Harvey, licensee of the Cross Keys Inn was charged with permitting drunkenness on his premises in 1908. It came about after Charles Till, a boat-loader who lived on the Cannock Road, was found lying on the footpath by P.C. Willis. Despite being a cold December night, Till was so drunk that he was unable to stagger the last few yards to his house, instead he had to be carried home on a stretcher.

It emerged that Till had spent the entire afternoon and evening at the inn and thought he had consumed about ten pints of beer. He was fined a shilling plus costs and made to pay for "damage done to the stretcher" - we can only speculate how this might have been caused! Mr Harvey was landed with a much more painful £10 fine plus costs.

Enoch Shire, an elderly labourer, claimed that he had only had two or three half-pints when he was collared for being drunk and disorderly in Church Street in 1914. He said that when he got out into the fresh air the drink "got over" him. Two shillings was deemed a sufficient penalty.

Heavy drinking was not the exclusive domain of men in the village - there were plenty of women who were just as enthusiastic in their consumption of alcohol and the raucous behaviour that inevitably followed.

In the year before the Great War, there were several drink-related disturbances at Tan Yard. In mid 1913, Frank and Sarah Rodwell were summoned for using bad language at their house in the Yard but according to Mr Rodwell, it was "only a bit of a family affair". He claimed that it seemed loud because the walls were only one brick thick and being near water made it seem louder still (!). A fine and costs were imposed.

Mary Jane Hartwell and her mother Mary Jane Rotchell were summoned for using obscene language in May of the same year and both were fined 18 shillings. The following month Hartwell and Fanny Elsmore were both described as "mad with drink" at Tan Yard at about 11:30pm. Constable Woolley said he was called to a disturbance involving Hartwell and her mother and also found Elsmore staggering about the road. When he told Elsmore to go home she at first refused, telling him "keep your hair on". She soon acquiesced and went indoors but a minute or two later she re-emerged and ran screaming across the street!

Elsmore's husband told the court that she had been neglecting him, their house and their children and he didn't know what to do. Both women were ordered to pay costs and agreed to 'sign the pledge', that is, to agree to abstain from drink.

Two other members of the Elsmore clan, brothers William and George, were brought to court for disorderly behaviour at a sports day, held in a field beside the Cannock Road. The Ancient Order of Foresters staged this annual event to raise money for their charitable causes but on this occasion it was badly disrupted by the Elsmores and a couple of other miners.

After being denied entry to the beer tent, it was alleged that George Elsmore threatened a competitor and began swearing profusely, while William got into the enclosure and caused a fracas. Sergeant Woolley meticulously noted down all that George Elsmore had shouted out and when shown the transcript, Elsmore told the officer "you would make a good editor"! The event came to a standstill, as spectators flocked to the incident, while another police officer and the sports referee tried to diffuse the situation. Despite their "disgraceful conduct", those involved were fined quite lightly as no serious offence had been committed.

In April of the following year, Mrs Elsmore and Gertrude Handley were summoned for using bad language at Elsmore's house in Mill Street. When Constable Wallis told them he was going to report the pair, they told him to "get on with it" adding "we don't care". Lord Hatherton said it was "perfectly horrible" that women should use such language and fined them both.

In May, Hartwell was once more before the bench, this time for fighting with her husband's friend outside her house. Hartwell's husband had come home drunk with a couple of friends in tow and one of them, Frank Kenerdine, hung around outside, spoiling for a fight with anyone. Hartwell opened his window and told Kenerdine to go home but he continued to hang about. When Mrs Hartwell came to the door and told him to clear off, the pair came to blows and ended up scrapping on the floor. Hartwell claimed Kenerdine knocked her down, at which she cried out "murder" and sent her mother, Mrs Rotchell, for the police. Kenerdine claimed that Hartwell struck the first blow and the pair then fell to the ground.

It was patently obvious to the Bench that it was 'six of one and half a dozen of the other' - both were fined five shillings and ordered to split the costs.

In addition to spontaneous 'punch-ups', the area has also seen organised fights in the past. Calf Heath was used as a venue for prize-fighting throughout the eighteenth and nineteenth centuries, no doubt because its comparatively remote location was easily accessible from Watling Street, and later, the railway. There are a number of newspaper reports of such contests, with participants and spectators coming on to the Heath from the Green Dragon at Hatherton and from Four Ashes Station.

These illicit contests sometimes attracted huge crowds and large amounts of money were wagered. The police would sometimes get wind of an event and turn up en masse to arrest the contestants, organisers and those 'making a book'. Newspapers often carried reports of the contests and the police action, the ensuing chaos caused by the latter often making much better reading than the reports of the fights themselves!

There are also instances of these bare-knuckle contests at various venues in Penkridge itself; in the spring of 1775 for example, Reynolds of Drayton and Crutchley of Dunston met at the King's Arms in front of an enormous crowd. The battle was described as "a severe contest" lasting for some fifteen minutes and was said by those present to have been the best that had been fought there for many years.

Meat, Fish and Poaching

Until the introduction of trading standards and sanitary inspections, selling adulterated food or meat unfit for human consumption, was not uncommon. If a farmer wanted to water down milk, a grocer bulk up his tea with sawdust or a butcher sell a joint that was well past its best, there was no-one to protect the hapless customer from being duped (and possibly poisoned!) other than himself. In smaller communities, such as Penkridge, shopkeepers and other vendors tended to be much more circumspect about their actions, as the faintest whiff of wrong-doing could destroy their business overnight.

Nevertheless, it seems that a few people were prepared to bend the rules; Market Square butcher Edmund Gilbert for example, was fined £10 plus costs in spring 1880 for selling two sheep carcases which were unfit for human consumption.

Another Market Street butcher, Horace Caspar Stellard, was summoned by Cannock Council inspectors in 1903 for having diseased meat at his premises. The inspector visited Mr Stellard's slaughterhouse in mid-February and found the carcases of a bullock, two pigs, a sheep and a quantity of other meat, all dressed and ready for sale. One of the pigs was found to be diseased and decaying, with the carcase emitting a strong smell.

In his defence, Stellard said that the pig had been killed by local farmer John Bedford who had brought it to him to see if it was suitable for consumption. He decided that it was not and placed it in the slaughterhouse temporarily until he had time to dispose of it. Mr Bedford's evidence backed up the butcher's account and the case was dismissed.

Another local butcher, Edward James Meredith, tried a different, but unsuccessful, tack to increase profits. He was sentenced to 12 months plus hard labour for stealing sheep from local farms - he was arrested after brazenly driving four stolen sheep through the village in broad daylight!

George Taylor, a fishmonger of Market Street was summoned to the Petty Sessions by the district council Sanitary Inspector. The official, Mr Whitehouse, recounted how he had bought some bloaters from Taylor's shop on 31st October 1899, but found them to be unfit for human consumption. He returned to the premises, seized two boxes of fish and had them destroyed. Mr Taylor incurred a fine and costs of over eighteen shillings.

Taking animals that belong to someone else, or taking wild animals from land belonging to someone else, like drunkenness and mis-selling, has no doubt gone on since time out of mind. Although no less a crime than any other form of theft, it is easy to sympathise with the unemployed labourer who might have taken the odd pheasant or rabbit to feed his starving family. For others though, poaching was nothing but a way of making money and they frequently went armed, with no compunction about using their weapons against whoever should try to stop them.

William Hall of 'The Foxholes', was brought before the Bench in January 1869 in connection with rabbit-trapping on land beside the Wolverhampton Road, occupied by Mr Croydon. He was fined 2s 6d with costs of 10s, or a fortnight in jail in default. William Price was given nine months imprisonment with hard labour for poaching and assaulting a gamekeeper on Mr Hellier's land.

George Lakin (17) and Albert Choyce (19), both of Dunston Heath, were described by Mr Perry at Penkridge Petty Sessions as a pair of notorious poachers, despite their youth. Lakin had been convicted ten times before for the same offence and Choyce, nice times. When they appeared before Mr Perry in June 1882 they had only just come out of prison, having each served a month for night poaching. For the offence now before the court, Lakin was fined 40 shillings or a further month in prison and Choyce, who did not appear, was given a month with hard labour.

Two years later the pair were back in court again, this time charged with carrying unlicensed guns. In view of their 'previous', they were each fined £5 plus costs.

Not exactly poaching, but eighteen-year-old sawyer Charles Waltho, was sentenced to three weeks with hard labour for stealing a chicken from wheelwright John Shutt. Mr Shutt, who lived near the Spread Eagle, was watching the young man as he worked and saw him take a fowl from the yard into an adjacent field.

Rather than question the young man, he reported the matter to the police and that evening, keeping close watch, Inspector Pike saw the accused enter the field. Having picked up the the dead bird, Waltho jumped over a hedge into the road, where the Inspector lay in wait.

In addition to theft of crops and livestock, farmers often had to deal with their animals being attacked, especially by dogs. A typical case of sheep worrying took place at Gailey Lea Farm in 1911. The farmer's son saw two dogs attacking a number of sheep and immediately called his father. Mr Tomlinson managed to drive off the dogs, wounding one of them with his shotgun. In a brilliant piece of detective work, Sergeant Woolley and Constable Williams managed to trace the dogs to a house in Hednesford but no account is given of the outcome. In all, five sheep had been injured, two having their back legs completely bitten off and their throats torn away.

Miscellanea

Let us end this chapter on a lighter note, with a few funny or interesting news snippets, before delving into the matter of death and destruction in Penkridge's past...

Walter Rowley of Rugeley was fined £1 6s for stealing a ferret from a Penkridge rat-catcher in 1839. In time-honoured tradition, Rowley claimed he had "bought it off a man" near the village, although he didn't go as far as saying "in a pub".

A monster pike was pulled from the Penk in the summer of 1877. Mr Malpass of Wolverhampton was the lucky angler although he required the assistance of a bystander to finally land the fish. It weighed in at over 18 pounds, was 3 feet 6 inches long and over 16 inches maximum girth!

There are several instances of lads being brought to court for throwing stones in Victorian Penkridge. Young Watley Wakelam, who worked at Dunston Hall as a groom, appeared before the Petty Sessions in June 1890, a prosecution being brought on behalf of the London & North Western Railway. He had taken advantage of a nice evening to sit on the parapet of the railway bridge at Dunston, armed with a selection of stones. As a Crewe to Bushbury goods train passed beneath, Wakelam launched his missiles, one of which bounced off the engine tender and another hit the guard's van. When the train arrived at Penkridge it was found that one of the van's windows had been broken.

A young woman named Cooper, who was nearby at the time of the incident, was called as a witness. She said that she saw the accused throwing stones and Wakelam himself later admitted having done so. A seemingly trivial act led to the young man being committed to the next Assizes at Stafford.

Six years later, a nine-year-old lad from Bishops Wood was brought to the Petty Sessions for throwing stones at a pony. The creature took fright, stumbled, and as a consequence injured itself, as well as being badly cut by one of the stones. The story is included here not because of the act itself but because of the punishment meted out to the boy. Lord Hatherton said that the law did not allow him to order the boy to be whipped but if his mother, who was in court, would administer the birch there and then, the Bench would consider the matter concluded. No mention is made in reports of the case at to whether or not the punishment was carried out.

In the year before the Great War, the parents of five lads aged between nine and twelve were each fined three shillings after their sons were summoned for throwing stones at telegraph pole insulators - a 'game' that was still popular until at least the 1960s!

Sometimes even the most innocuous activity could land the participants in court; just before the end of Victoria's reign, five lads were fined for throwing snowballs in Church Lane. We can only guess that they were targeting windows, or perhaps the local vicar rather than each other!

Chapter 2 - Accidents & Deaths

Unexplained and Unfortunate Deaths

A sudden death was recorded at Penkridge Wharf in January 1798. A boatman who had been carrying on some business with the wharfinger (the wharf manager), was heading back to his vessel when he discovered he had left his stick behind. On returning to the office he found the man he had been talking to seconds beforehand completely lifeless, with a pen still clasped in his hand!

A woman and her daughter, gathering heather on Calf Heath one April day in 1826, found the body of a man lying face down. An inquest was held at the Four Ashes Inn, where it was determined that the man was Samuel Bennett, a Dudley shoe-mender, who had travelled to Stafford to buy some materials for his trade. The inquest heard that on his return journey, Mr Bennett took a wagon that went as far as the Spread Eagle, and a woman who rode with him said he was very much the worse for drink. She gave him directions to the Four Ashes and that was the last she saw of him.

The witness said that Mr Bennett had some leather and a cobbler's 'last' in a bundle, money in his pocket and a handkerchief around his neck. When his body was found, there was no trace of the handkerchief, his money or his possessions. As there was no sign of violence and Mr Bennett had in the last year or so suffered two strokes or fits, the jury had little option but to give a verdict of "found dead".

On 24th February 1860 the body of a baby girl was found in the canal and an inquest was duly conducted at the Boat Inn. A post mortem showed that the body of the month-old child had been in the water for several days and that she died as a result of a blow to the head. Since there was no clue as to the parents of the child, the inquest was adjourned for a week to enable police to make further enquiries but whether they had any success is not known.

A similarly grisly find had been made in the vicinity about eight years earlier, when the body of a male infant was found in a pile of manure at Calf Heath, although on this occasion the body was in a badly decomposed state. An inquest was held at Penkridge but a verdict is not noted in the press; given the level of forensic science available at this date, it seems unlikely that the cause of death could have been accurately determined in any case.

The body of a tramp was discovered beneath a straw rick beside the Stafford Road, about a quarter of a mile from the village, in late November 1864. The poor fellow had no boots, stockings or shirt and the body was in a shocking state, with one eye and parts of his face and hands eaten by vermin. An inquest was held at the George and Fox, where a verdict of death due to cold and starvation was returned.

On Friday 31st October 1884 an inquest was held at the same inn upon the body of an unknown man, thought to be around 35 years of age. The man had lodged at the house of Mrs Oakley in the village but she didn't know his name. He was next seen at a house at Dunston Heath where he stopped to ask for help, but shortly afterwards he collapsed and died. "Death from natural causes" was the verdict, despite the comparative youth of the man.

Nineteen-year-old Arthur Talbot suffered that most unlucky fate - being struck and killed by lightning. He and a few other men were hoeing turnips at Otherton Farm in 1893 when a violent summer thunderstorm descended upon the area. The workers had all taken shelter beneath a tree, when Talbot and an older man, Edward Dawson, were struck by the same bolt of lightning. The younger man died as a result of the extensive burns to his thighs and chest but Dawson lived to tell the tale.

James Eccleshall, a fourteen-year-old of Clay Street, died as a result of digging potatoes. He caught his toe with the garden fork he was using and although the wound healed, he died about two weeks later, as a result of tetanus. The inquest, held in August 1911, returned a verdict of accidental death, the coroner remarking that it was a "sad end from such a simple act".

Considerable excitement was aroused in the area following the death of a shepherd, employed by local farmer Mr Keeling, in 1855. Joseph Day, who was about sixty years of age, was said to have taken some 'quack medicine', which the seller claimed could cure virtually every illness known to mankind.

Mr Day appeared to be in good health when he attended a Friendly Society meeting at the Jockey on a Thursday evening, but after taking a few drops of the 'medicine' on Saturday, he died.

The con-man who sold him this wonder drug had been staying at Stafford for a month or more. In addition to his potions, he offered cures for a similarly wide range of ailments for anyone prepared to pay to be hooked up to his “electric galvanic battery”.

More than one person had died at Stafford as a result of taking the medicine, although the inquest on Day, held at the Crown Inn, was inconclusive. It was noted however, that the skin of his chest and stomach were strangely discoloured.

Cart and Carriage Accidents

Given the omnipresence of horse and cart up until the early 20th century, it is hardly surprising that they were often the cause of accidents, frequently resulting in serious injury or death.

In the spring of 1823, a Coppenhall farmer named Sayer was leading his horse and cart through Penkridge when the horse took fright. In an attempt to restrain the animal, the unfortunate man fell down and a cartwheel passed over him. He must have suffered serious internal injuries as his body was dreadfully bruised and he died on the evening of the following day.

In 1857 Richard Bellamore, a thirty-year-old wagoner who worked for Lord Hatherton, suffered a fatal accident as he was about to start work. It was 5am and he had just got his wagon and two horses ready to fetch a load of sheep. It seems that the horses suddenly took fright and, as he tried to restrain them, Bellamore was caught between his vehicle and the wall of the wagon shed. Although no-one witnessed the event, it was possible to deduce what had happened from heavy scoring on the wall, made by the nave of the wagon's wheel. Poor Bellamore's right arm was badly broken and his head was terribly crushed.

Bellamore, his wife and four young children lived at New Building, Teddesley Hay and he had worked on the same farm since he was a boy. A coroner's inquest was held at Teddesley Farm in the afternoon of the same day, leading to a verdict of accidental death.

In February 1863, seventy year old labourer Daniel Tarlington, who worked for John Lees of Drayton, was knocked down by his own horse and cart; the wheel ran over him and he was killed outright.

In 1864, Walter Lees was also run over by his own wagon. The victim and his colleague, Joseph Evans, were bringing a cart-load of soot from Wolverhampton, and as they were passing out of the village, Lees stumbled and fell under the wheels of the cart with the usual results. The inquest, hearing that he was a sober and steady man, returned a verdict of accidental death.

The cargo in this incident may seem rather odd, but in those days, all sorts of refuse was carted out of towns and spread onto fields. Human waste was referred to as 'night-soil' since it was not permitted to move it during the day for obvious reasons!

A similar accident occurred 20 years later, when 71-year-old Thomas Weatherer, an agricultural labourer of Mill Street, ended up under his cart. One afternoon in June, he was seen leading his horses across a field, with a cart-load of two tons of stone. The unfortunate man must have stumbled soon after, as a man named Hodgkiss heard him cry out and saw him beneath the wheels of the cart. Hodgkiss managed to extricate the old man and had him sent home, but a fractured spine and other injuries lead to his death a few hours later. The inquest, held at the Star Inn, returned a verdict of accidental death.

Albert Dyke, landlord of the Lord Nelson Inn, suffered a fatal accident while unloading wheat at his father's farm at Dunston. He fell from a wagon and a prong of the fork that he was using entered his right eye to a depth of two inches. The poor man lived on for almost two months before passing away from this ghastly injury - he was just twenty five years of age.

Local magistrate Frederick Charles Perry, of Dunston Hall, suffered a serious head injury in 1873 when he was thrown from his horse. He was conducting some business from horseback at Penkridge Wharf in February of that year, when his mount took fright, throwing him against a nearby wall. It was feared that the blow would prove fatal but Mr Perry recovered and continued to serve the community for many years thereafter.

In 1901, well respected Market Street grocer Richard B. Jones suffered a fatal accident upon his return home from Codsall on a foggy November evening. When near the vicarage, one wheel of his trap ran up a bank and the unfortunate man was pitched head-first onto the road. Sixty-two-year old Mr Jones died almost instantly from a broken neck.

His body and the overturned trap were discovered by local postman Edwin Oakley, making his way home from his round. Following an inquest at the Horse & Jockey, the coroner returned a verdict of accidental death. The funeral at St Michael's was attended by a large number of people and there was a considerable outpouring of grief and expressions of sympathy from mourners who had come from near and far.

Murder and Suicide

In June 1791, local eighteen-year-old, Martha North, cut the throat of a four-year-old girl who died shortly afterwards. No other detail is given but it was supposed that the attack happened as result of temporary insanity because North had previously been very affectionate to the child.

Ann Saunders was arrested for the suspected murder of her illegitimate child at Penkridge in 1783. She confessed to the act when questioned, saying that she had buried the infant in her garden. The body was soon recovered and the woman committed for trial.

In 1856, mother and daughter, Elizabeth and Martha Guest were charged with the murder of Martha's illegitimate child, Mary Elizabeth Derry, in May of the previous year. The case excited considerable interest in the village, especially as the women were 'respectably connected' - Martha's sister being married to a notable Liverpool tradesman - although Elizabeth's husband and sons were all farm labourers.

Twenty-five-year-old Martha Guest worked as a servant to a Wolverhampton publican by the name of Derry, a man in his mid-fifties, and had become pregnant by him. She left his employment soon after and gave birth to the child at Wolverhampton in February 1855, at the home of a man named Whittall. Elizabeth Guest agreed to look after the child, provided that Derry paid over £20 towards its upkeep, and she took the baby back to Penkridge when it was just three weeks old.

A woman named Hannah Dyer, who lived with Whittall as his housekeeper and mistress, told the Petty Sessions that she had seen Martha and the baby in Wolverhampton and the child seemed perfectly healthy but it had become ill soon after. When Dyer tried to arrange to see the child, she was told that mother and baby had gone to Liverpool. In spite of this, a week or so later Dyer travelled to Penkridge and when she mentioned the matter in passing to the toll-gate keeper upon arrival, she was shocked to hear that the child was dead and buried.

Dyer went to the Guest household but didn't ask Martha about the baby until the pair went out for a walk, at which point Martha broke down and confirmed that the child was dead. She said that she wanted to tell Hannah about it, but her mother forbade it. It seems that Whittall thought the circumstances very suspicious and it was at his instigation that the body was subsequently exhumed and a coroner's inquest held.

The hearing at Penkridge, held before a packed courtroom, lasted for some six hours and Martha Guest broke down on several occasions. After hearing all the evidence, both prisoners were returned to custody and committed for trial at the Assizes.

When they appeared at Stafford, it was revealed that Elizabeth Guest had taken the infant to a local doctor when it had become poorly, and he prescribed some powders for it. She subsequently took it to a Mrs Saunders in the village, who 'prescribed' Magnesia for it. Neither had any effect and the baby died less than two weeks later.

A post mortem revealed minute traces of the poisonous metal Antimony in the child's stomach but the cause of death was a blood clot on the brain. The prosecution alleged that this was caused by a blow from a blunt instrument, whereas Mrs Guest, who was described as very feeble and suffering deep mental anxiety in court, claimed that the child had died from "water in the head".

The judge directed the jury to consider the matter very carefully and only to convict if they were certain beyond all reasonable doubt that one of the defendants had struck the child a mortal blow. In view of that fact that there was no discernible motive for the alleged crime, the jury returned a not guilty verdict against both women.

Lest we view Mr Derry too harshly, it emerged in court that in addition to the £20 initially handed over, he had also given money to Elizabeth Guest to help her buy a horse, to Martha to help her in finding another job, and had agreed to provide further money to support the child as and when required.

Within a few years, Martha guest had moved away to London. By 1861, and now nearly thirty, she was living at Rotherhithe, still unmarried and still working as a domestic servant.

In 1868 Jane Howard, a poor single woman who had recently moved to Penkridge and lived in a hut at Fox-Holes, was arrested on suspicion of the murder of her newly born child. The infant's body had been discovered in a parcel under a hedge near Rickerscote and the police were said to have strong evidence that she was the mother. Once again, no record of a trial is reported in the available newspapers.

Richard and Louisa Brindley were held in custody following a suspected child murder at Penkridge in 1896. The pair were involved in 'baby farming', that is, taking unwanted infants in exchange for money, usually from young single women.

The pair had been questioned on a similar charge at Birkenhead – in that case having apparently taken an unwanted child for cash and subsequently abandoned it. The baby was found in a shop doorway and subsequently died.

While living at Penkridge, it seems that they took in a baby from Mary Workman of Dudley, who paid them almost £10 and signed an agreement, giving up any claim to the child. When questioned, the Brindleys maintained that they had given the baby to a doctor's wife in Wolverhampton.

The Brindleys appeared at Penkridge on a charge of wilful murder of the child but no evidence was offered and they were remanded to Stafford, to be returned to Liverpool to face a lesser charge in connection with the Birkenhead case. Whether they ever appeared in court on that charge is not known.

There are few reported suicides in Penkridge in the nineteenth century. However, we do have to keep in mind that suicide was still a criminal offence, which may have deterred many from attempting it – failure could result in the 'double whammy' of further anguish and a criminal conviction to boot!

Elizabeth Woollams, wife of a labourer who lived at Boscomoor, cut her own throat with a razor in 1799. The inquest held at the Littleton Arms returned a verdict of 'lunacy' or temporary insanity. A local groom, George Price, was less successful when using the same method on Boxing Day 1862. He was charged with attempting to commit suicide but the bench seemed content with his expression of regret and his promise not to repeat the episode; he was let off with a stern reprimand.

Christmas of the following year was not a happy time for Eli

Higgins, landlord of the Boat Inn. He had been very low and melancholy for some time and a week into the new year he took his own life. He left the table at tea without eating or drinking and went out, supposedly for a walk. In fact he had gone into an outbuilding at the inn, locked the door behind him, put the key in his pocket and hung himself. A brief search, conducted some hours after he had determined his fate, led to the discovery of his stone cold body.

A most extraordinary local suicide was that of 22-year-old Joseph Price, who took his own life on his wedding night in 1887. Price, a labourer of New Buildings Farm, married a young woman named Annie Crutchley and on the same evening, left his house never to return. After an extensive search his clothes were found, leading to the recovery of his body from the bottom of Trench Pit pool. No cause was given for his actions although it was said that his intellect was affected, especially in hot weather.

On Saturday 1st December 1870, an inquest was held at the Boat Inn on the body of Police Sergeant Jabez Rushton. Mr Rushton, who left a widow and seven children, was a much respected member of the community, having served the folk of Penkridge for fourteen years by the time of his death.

The inquest heard that he was last seen at Mr Rogers' house near Wolgarston Pool on Wednesday, and was going to see Mr Cook, Lord Hatherton's gamekeeper. His body was found in the pool, which was on his route to the gamekeeper's lodge, later in the evening.

There were two strange but possibly unrelated facts about the case. Firstly, it was said that Rushton had always had a distinct dislike of still or running water, such as pools or rivers and would not willingly have gone near them. Secondly, and perhaps more relevant, he had been called in by his superiors to explain his uncharacteristic absence from duty on the Monday evening before his death. The jury decided that this latter event must have been preying on his mind but whether it was a contributory factor in his death they could not decide and returned the oft used verdict of 'found drowned'.

Chapter 3 - Road, Rail & Water

On The Roads

With the opening of the Grand Junction Railway in 1837, the writing was on the wall for horse-drawn mail and passenger coaches. It may be that one local entrepreneur saw what was coming well in advance, as twenty "powerful, well seasoned coach horses in capital condition" were sold by auction at the Littleton Arms in 1833. Included in the sale were three sets of harness and several blood colts.

Amongst the coaches running through Penkridge at this time were 'The Traveller', 'The Eclipse' and 'The Bang-Up' stopping at the Littleton Arms, while the 'Erin Go Bragh' (or 'Ireland Forever') and 'The Rocket' stopped at the George & Fox, and 'The Hark Forward' stopped at the White Hart.

We can get an idea of the laborious journey times involved by looking at the timetable of a typical mail coach, the twice daily Liverpool to Birmingham. The evening service set off at 6:30pm and was scheduled to arrive at the George & Fox at 4am. If the coach ended its journey on time at 6:45am, it would have travelled 100 miles in just over twelve hours, giving an average speed of about 8mph.

The Holyhead mail coach 'Regulator' met with an accident at Penkridge on Christmas morning 1835. The coach overturned completely, although none of its passengers were badly hurt and after being righted, it continued to Wolverhampton, arriving just an hour behind schedule.

Six young men were brought to the magistrates' court following a night-time prank in the summer of 1863. The caper caused the local mail cart to be delayed but would have led to much greater disruption had it occurred in the days of the old coach services.

The group had been drinking at the 'Jockey Club' and when they left at around 4am, decided it would be a good idea to block the turnpike road near the Post Office. To do so, they wheeled a timber-wagon out of the yard of Mr Gilbert, a local builder, and placed it squarely across the Wolverhampton Road. When the mail cart came along shortly afterwards, it was found necessary to obtain a horse to move the offending vehicle.

Sergeant Blakely had been witness to the final moments of the event, although only two of the group were seen to have actually touched the wagon. The unlucky pair received a fine and costs totalling 15 shillings each; the others were acquitted.

With the introduction of the bicycle, motor car and motorcycle, the police and courts had new offences to deal with, although some, such as failure to obtain a licence, missing lights, dangerous driving and so on, all had their equivalents in the horse-drawn era.

Dunston Heath farmer William Pedley was fined almost 10 shillings for driving without a light at Stone Cross in 1913 - after being stopped, he borrowed two lamps to enable him to continue on his way!

When John Ivins of Yew Tree Cottages was stopped by P.C. Wallis for riding his bike on Quarry Heath without a light, he came up with a bizarre excuse: he claimed he was unable to stop to light his lamp because he was travelling downhill with his brother on the cross-bar. We can only assume that it got dark very quickly in May 1914 and that the officer was at the bottom of the hill!

Constable Wallis had less success when trying to stop eighteen-year-old Ada James of Preston Vale a year earlier - she completely ignored his calls to pull-up when he spotted her riding without lights. A village bobby would know everyone on his patch in those days and there was no escape for young Ada who was handed a ten shilling fine.

In September 1913, Joseph Braine, a Birmingham man, was heavily fined for "driving a motor car to the danger of the public". At court, numerous witnesses recounted how they had seen a 'cigar-shaped' car being driven along Watling Street, between Gailey and Longford, at speeds of up to 70 mph. Samuel Meanwell, who lived near the Four Crosses Inn, said the engine sounded like that of an aeroplane and that at times the wheels completely left the ground.

Isaac Hawksworth of Gailey said he heard what sounded like an aeroplane approaching but by the time he had dashed the 20 yards to his gate, nothing was to be seen in either direction, despite the fact that he could see three quarters of a mile along the road. A little later he saw the car passing by again and estimated its speed at about 70 mph.

Another man, Robert Knight, who was breaking stones at Gailey, saw the car pass by three or four times, on each occasion travelling at about 60 mph. A carter said the car passed him three times as he travelled some 350 yards along the road past the Plough Inn with his load of straw.

It transpired that Mr Braine was a test-driver for the experimental department of the Wolseley Motor Company of Birmingham. In his defence, he claimed that he had been testing the working of the carburettors and had not exceeded 35 mph on any of his ‘runs’. Furthermore, he said that it would be impossible to obtain a much higher speed speed from this particular vehicle. The bench decided that even 35 mph was dangerous, given the number of crossroads along that stretch of road, and imposed over £9 in fines and costs and endorsed his licence.

Although steam engines could travel at greater speeds in this era, it must have been quite shocking to see a road vehicle being driven at such a rate, especially given its novel form and exceptionally loud engine. Exactly why Braine was testing the engine so far from the company’s works in Birmingham is not known.

A couple of months earlier, Penkridge postman Edward Henry Brookes was fined 2s 6d for riding his bicycle without a light. He claimed that he was not actually riding it as he only had one foot on the pedals!

Pillaton farmer Robert Heath failed to pay road tax on his motorcycle for almost two years from 1907, yet he had used the machine almost every day during that time. Imposing a fine and costs of over one pound, Lord Hatherton said no wonder rate-payers were complaining, when they were being defrauded of the money that such licences were designed to bring in.

There are many cases of cyclists being fined for riding on the pavement around the end of the 19th century, when cycling was extremely popular and groups of cyclists would often travel many tens of miles on day trips. One such case was brought at Penkridge in the summer of 1890, when five men from Wolverhampton, Wednesbury and Birmingham were fined between five and ten shillings each. They said that the roads were so poor that they had no alternative but to use the pavement – a claim that was made by many other cyclists who ended up in court around this time. Lord Hatherton said that if the road surface was that dangerous they should dismount and walk until it was safe to set off once more.

John Wallace and Aaron Hodkiss, two broom (or 'besom') makers who lived next to each other on Market Street, were each fined 11s 6d for allowing their horses to stray onto the highway in 1884, an offence which neither denied. John Wallace later became a scrap dealer in the village, as mentioned elsewhere.

Female butchers are not often encountered today or in the past, but in 1866 Sarah Wilton carried on the trade at Penkridge. On 29th March of that year she was fined two shillings and sixpence for conveying a cow's feet and belly on the public highway without a licence!

In November 1900 John Pugh of Wolverhampton was fined three shillings and sixpence plus costs for obstructing the highway. He had left his two horses and dray unsupervised outside one of the local pubs for three quarters of an hour.

Just before the Great War, a traction engine driver was fined for taking water from a hydrant in the village. The man, who worked for Collins' circus, was on his way from Wolverhampton to Stafford when he discovered he was running short of water. Police Constable Wallis told the court that he was walking along Wolverhampton Road when the driver drew up alongside and asked where he could obtain water. Wallis directed him to the river, but coming upon him near Bull Bridge a little later, he found that the man had prised off the cap of a hydrant and was filling his boiler via a hose.

Harry Prosser, the locomotive driver, told the court Chairman that he thought his employer had a contract with the South Staffordshire Water Company and he was therefore entitled to top up wherever he chose. He said he regularly used the hydrants at Wolverhampton and Stafford and didn't deny using that at Penkridge. His excuse for not taking water from the Penk was that he didn't like the thought of his engine remaining upon the bridge - a valid argument given the state of some bridges and the weight of these behemoths. Taking water from a hydrant was nevertheless an offence and he was fined five pounds plus costs.

With the founding of the RSPCA in the 1830s, the welfare of animals, especially livestock and horses was much better protected than had formerly been the case. Despite the fact that many people relied upon their animals for their livelihood, there are many cases of ponies and horses being worked when they were in a totally unsatisfactory condition.

For example, in 1884, Henry Lewis, a wagoner of Mitton, and his employer Thomas Haynes, were both brought before the court for working five horses with bad sores on their shoulders. Haynes claimed that the wounds were boils, rather than sores caused by mistreatment. The case was brought after observation by an

RSPCA inspector (literally, in the field) and separate observations by Sergeant Price in the village. The court did not agree with Haynes' assertions and both men were fined.

In 1912 Samuel Cockayne, a miner who lived in a caravan, was summoned for ill-treating a donkey. Constable Wallace spotted a number of raw wounds on the animal's back, as it pulled a cart-load of firewood through the village. The wounds were covered with a black substance which the officer thought was intended to hide them but which Cockayne claimed was Vaseline, applied to help the wounds heal.

The court heard that the donkey was otherwise in reasonable condition and decided that the man be allowed to keep it upon payment of a small fine and provided that the RSPCA inspector could see it before it was once again put it to work.

Another frequently reported transgression connected with the roads was that of discharging a firearm within 50 feet of the highway, and in the summer of 1887, David Dagley was accused of doing just that.

He was standing in a field beside Congreve Lane when he saw a hare running along the middle of the carriageway and he instinctively took a shot at it. In court he claimed that the creature was being pursued by Constable Emineson and his dog and, although he knew he was in the wrong, he was “not going to let a thing like that get past me”!

Constable Emineson said he was at least sixty yards behind the hare but whether he was chasing it or not was irrelevant according to the bench and Dagley was handed a small fine and costs.

Rail Chaos

The Grand Junction Railway opened in 1837, just three years after the contract for the Penkridge section had been put out to tender by the famous railway engineer George Stephenson. It was one of the first major railway routes in the world and it had an immediate impact on village life, allowing goods and people to flow in and out as never before.

Within a few years of opening, passengers could travel almost the length and breadth of the country, in journey times that would have seemed unbelievable just a few decades earlier. Although the first passenger carriages were little more than open-air cattle trucks with bench seating, conditions gradually improved, and within twenty years comparatively comfortable coaches were the norm and passenger travel boomed.

In one of the earliest accidents on the newly constructed Grand Junction Railway, a 14-year-old youth by the name of Robert Foster was killed near Penkridge when he fell beneath the wheels of a wagon carrying stone.

Less than a year later, there was a terrible collision between a mixed (goods and passenger) train from Penkridge to Stafford and the locomotive 'Caliban'. Two tenders and two empty horse boxes between the locomotive and the passenger coach were said to have prevented any loss of life, despite the violence of the collision. Both drivers were pitched off their engines and the Caliban became a runaway, racing off at great speed and running twelve miles before running out of steam.

The accident was attributed to the fact that the Penkridge train had arrived some twenty minutes before it was due - not an unusual occurrence in those early days when timetables were quite fluid and signalling almost non-existent!

There was a collision between two passenger trains near Penkridge station on Christmas Eve 1852. Delays had been building up throughout the day across the Midlands, due to a combination of overwhelming passenger numbers and speed restrictions in certain places, caused by recent flooding. As a result, lines, junctions and stations were very congested.

An evening London to Manchester train had just left the station and was getting up to speed, when a Shropshire Union train from Wolverhampton ploughed into the back of it. Whether the driver of the latter had misread the signals on the south side of the station, or whether he was unable to stop due to the slippery rails wasn't clear, but his engine seriously damaged the last two coaches of the leading train. Although there were no fatalities, many people suffered broken bones and others had serious cuts and bruises.

An equally serious accident occurred to a train near Dunston in 1861, when the ash box, located beneath the locomotive's firebox, became detached and fouled the rails. The train, travelling north at about 40 mph was shaken violently for some considerable time, causing many of the timbers holding the coaches together to separate.

Eventually, engine and tender were tossed into the air, finally bringing the whole train to a stop. An inspector who happened to be aboard sent a man back down the line to Penkridge to warn the Stationmaster, while he himself proceeded towards Stafford on foot to raise the alarm there. Miraculously, no passenger suffered anything more than cuts and bruises but many carriages and the engine were severely damaged.

An express train from Liverpool to Birmingham stopped at Stafford on the evening of 4th October 1864, and four wagons, carrying parts of a merry-go-round, swing-boats and other fairground equipment were inserted between the engine and the passenger carriages. The train continued on its journey, but not too long after leaving Penkridge, it became evident that the newly added cargo was on fire. Flames and clouds of smoke fanned by the wind formed a most alarming sight, but the driver decided that stopping in this rural location would be a dangerous proposition as there was no prospect of summoning help to fight the blaze. Instead he pressed on with all speed to Wolverhampton, by which time the passengers had become fully aware, and no doubt completely terrified, of the inferno ahead of them.

As the train entered the station, furiously blowing its whistle, many passengers decided to take their chance and leapt from their coaches onto the platform. The train was brought to a halt just beyond the station, where the trucks were bravely detached and shunted into a siding.

Worked by a stiff breeze, the flames now grew to enormous height and it was feared that nearby warehouses would become engulfed before the fire could be brought under control. In the end, the fire was contained and miraculously, none of the passengers suffered anything more than minor injuries.

In the following year there was another accident at Penkridge, where passengers were once again lucky to escape with their lives. On this occasion the mail train from Birmingham ran into a brake van which had been left on the main line near the station, rather than being shunted into a siding. The majority of passengers were severely concussed but none suffered broken bones.

In 1902, a 92-year-old man was run down by a passenger train at Penkridge Station. Samuel Smith needed to get from one platform to another, and as there was no footbridge or underpass, he crossed the rails. Just as he was about to mount the desired platform he was hit by the speeding express and killed instantly, his body being terribly mangled.

The Parish Council, along with other organisations and individuals had repeatedly petitioned the railway company to install proper crossing facilities but their pleas had fallen on deaf ears - a staggering fact given that more than 120 trains passed through the station each day. Exactly the same type of accident happened on two occasions a little further down the line, at Four Ashes station.

Twenty-six-year-old railway shunter James Lane, a native of Stamford, Lincolnshire, was the victim of a most shocking accident at the station in December 1869. As was common practice, he was running beside a number of wagons when he signalled for the engine driver to slow down, and thereby slacken the coupling, so that it could be unhooked. Unfortunately, because he had not fastened the chain correctly in the first place, the free end swung out and fouled a points lever. Lane was tripped-up by the obstacle which had been unexpectedly thrown across his path and he fell under the wheels of one of the trucks.

The wagon ran across Lane's thigh and two railway fog signals that were in his pocket exploded. As the train was now moving slowly he managed to pull himself partially clear, but the following wheel ran over his ankle. When assistance arrived, the poor fellow was put on the next train to Stafford and taken to the

Infirmary. In addition to his broken legs, he had a broken arm and internal injuries. He was adjudged by the surgeon to be in too fragile a condition to undergo any sort of operation and he died that same night.

There was a near-miss on the railway just north of Penkridge in 1874, when two horses ran on to the line as a train carrying Lord Dartmouth, Lord Wrottesley, Sir Charles Adderley and a number of magistrates was passing. Fortunately, the train just missed the animals, although the weight and speed of the locomotive in use may have prevented a derailment.

At one time, Gailey had its own railway station, located on the south side of Watling Street, and it was the scene of a tragic accident in 1881.

A seventeen year old name Wallace, who was a member of the Royal Engineers, was undertaking work along the railway for the Ordnance Survey. As he stepped aside to avoid a goods train from Penkridge, he unwittingly stepped into the path of an express from Wolverhampton. He was admitted to hospital suffering from serious internal injuries but no great hope was held out for his recovery.

Stephen Barnes (alias Lloyd) was convicted in 1892 of assaulting a woman at Brewood and sentenced to four months hard labour. As he was being put aboard the train at Penkridge, en route to Stafford Gaol, he managed to slip free from the handcuffs which shackled him to another prisoner. Constable Hollins gave chase as Barnes ran about a hundred yards along the track and then down the embankment into the fields. Hollins however, was a very fit officer and soon managed to run down his prisoner in a nearby lane. Barnes was conveyed to prison by the next available train.

Water Woes

Although Penkridge itself is a fair distance from Wolverhampton, the Penk was not immune to the effects of the population and industry upstream until more stringent environmental controls were put in place. In 1888, the Board of Guardians was told that many village rate-payers were complaining about the state of the river. It was said to be so polluted that cows could not drink from it, fish were poisoned by it and the smell was atrocious. In this particular instance, the source of the pollution was sewage from Wolverhampton; the Corporation of that town fully acknowledged that they were responsible, but they seemed powerless to control it, despite having recently constructed a new sewage works at Barnfield, near Pendeford. It seems that the design or capacity of these works was inadequate, as there were numerous claims against the Corporation, from landowners and occupiers along the length of the river, after overspill of raw sewage onto their land.

At a local meeting in 1888, Mr Keeling, a respected farmer and civic dignitary, suggested that Wolverhampton Corporation might be inclined to act if the Board were to take action against them. Reverend Groom told those assembled that he understood that Wolverhampton was taking steps to deal with excess rainwater which would in turn remove the likelihood of overspill. In the end the Board decided to formally write to the Corporation, drawing their attention to the matter and hopefully eliciting some action.

Charles Williams, a married man from Birmingham, tried to commit suicide by jumping from the parapet of the railway viaduct into the river in 1869. He was spotted by Sergeant Rushton, who managed to drag him from the water and offer what resuscitation he could. Williams was unconscious for over an hour but thanks to the efforts of the policeman and others, he made a full recovery. Sadly, Mr Williams' woes did not end there, as attempted suicide was a criminal matter. He was brought before Captain Tudor at the Petty Sessions where he said that he had tried to end his life because he had not worked for a long time and was tired of life. At the pleading of his friends, who promised to look after him, he was discharged.

In July 1884, fourteen-year-old James Jeffreys of Swan Lane, was drowned in the Penk after falling into the river from a tree. It must have been a particularly unpleasant way to go, given the state of the Penk at this time, as mentioned above.

The Staffordshire and Worcestershire canal, opened in 1772, provided an enormous boost to business and industry throughout its length but it also gave rise to a large number of deaths, serious accidents and all sorts of crime. Given that there was no health and safety regulation, the inherently dangerous nature of locks and other infrastructure, and the inability of many people to swim, fatal accidents amongst canal workers and users were frequent. The canal also provided those looking for a 'way out' with a convenient means of ending their life.

In 1846, the Plough Inn, near Gailey, hosted an inquest into the death of John Mills, a boatman's assistant, who was drowned in Rodbaston lock. Mills was sent forward to open the lock but as he had been gone longer than expected, the captain went to see what was wrong; he found Mills' cap floating in the lock and his body was recovered soon after. As there was no sign of injury, the inquest jury returned a verdict of 'found drowned', making the assumption that Mills had simply fallen in while attempting to close the upper gate.

Another canal-related inquest was held at the Plough Inn during 1849, although this time drowning was not the cause of death. Sixty-year-old Kidderminster boatman John Kendall was clearing his tow-line over one of the paddles on the lock gate when his horse suddenly started forwards and the tow-rope struck him violently across the abdomen. He was put in the cabin and taken onwards to Gailey wharf but gradually deteriorated and succumbed to his internal injuries a little over a day later. It is interesting to note that his 'mate' was his sixty three year old wife.

Over half a century later, the Plough was the scene of another inquest but on this occasion it concerned a body recovered from the reservoir at Gailey rather than the canal. Arriving at the scene of the tragedy, Sergeant Woolley searched the man's pockets and found a pocket diary containing a poignant message to the man's mother.

"Dear Mother, I can't stand this any longer as my head is splitting. Do not worry for me but look after yourself. Give my best love to the kiddies and Annie and Art. Goodbye to all - From your broken-hearted Jack."

'Jack' was twenty-nine-year-old John Thomas of Hednesford. His stepfather told the inquest that the young man had given up work about two months earlier, complaining of pains in his head. Although he had been seen by a doctor, he had become more and more dispirited and depressed. He said that Jack had no reason to visit the Gailey area and the inquest decided that he must have gone there with the express intent of taking his own life. "Suicide whilst temporarily insane" was the verdict.

William Corker was taking a boat-load of ironstone from Etruria to Bilston in November 1836, when he passed through Penkridge.

Boatmen often travelled with their entire families and William was no exception, being accompanied by his wife Anne and her two children from a previous marriage, Martha aged 7, and 3-year-old Elizabeth.

As they entered 'Rocky Lock' at Penkridge, husband and wife left the boat to operate the gates, leaving the children in the cabin. As the water began to rise one of the girls suddenly cried out and, looking into the lock, the couple discovered that the stern of the boat was caught on the lower gates, preventing it from rising and as a result rapidly filling with water. William let down the paddles at the top of the lock to prevent any more water from entering and shouted to Anne to raise the lower paddles to level the boat.

Rather than following her husband's instructions however, Anne panicked and leapt into the cabin in an effort to save the girls but at the second she landed, the boat sank. Despite the best efforts of William and those who came to help, it took twenty minutes before the three bodies could be recovered, by which time any hope of resuscitation had completely passed.

An inquest was held at the Boat Inn, where a verdict of accidental death was returned. The three bodies were interred in one grave and the good folk of Penkridge met the costs of the burial and looked after the needs of the bereaved husband.

Young William Bott was very fortunate that Mrs Hannah Marshall was close at hand when he fell into the canal in April 1889. With little thought for her own safety, she plunged into the water,and after considerable effort, managed to pull the six-year-old to safety. In honour of her selfless action, she was given an award by the Royal Humane Society.

As well as being an occasional scene of misfortune, canals have provided great pleasure and entertainment for many people over last two centuries and in 1902 the local canal must have been a sight to behold. A fishing contest organised by a Birmingham angler's club attracted no less than 1,300 members and their friends, brought in by two special trains. Unsurprisingly, strict rules had to be applied to ensure that most of the catch was returned to the water.

In addition to that time-honoured recreation of throwing stones, young boys and girls like nothing better than sliding around on ice. Sadly, it is all too easy to find cases where children have ventured onto thin ice and lost their lives as a result. There was such an incident at Penkridge in the winter of 1870. George Blower and James Cecil were on their way to school when tempted by an expanse of recently formed ice, but it gave way under nine-year-old Blower and he ended up in twelve feet of ice-cold water. By the time help arrived, in the form of a young man named Butler, a lifeless body was all that could be recovered.

Mr and Mrs Maullin of Gailey had a narrow escape from warmer water while out visiting in their horse-drawn chaise in the summer of 1802. They pulled over at Calf Heath to let their horse drink from an old brick-kiln pit when, having sated its thirst, the animal stepped forward, only to plunge into a deep hole hidden beneath the surface. Horse and carriage all but disappeared and the couple had to clamber up onto the seat of the vehicle to keep their heads above water.

Fortunately, Mr Maullin was able to swim, and having made the bank, ran to a nearby farmhouse to get help in rescuing his wife.

Chapter 4 - Domestic & Other Crimes

Family Matters

Look back into the past of any village and you'll probably find one or two notorious individuals or families who form a blight on the area for a period of time, often for just a few years. Sometimes adolescent behaviour is the cause, other times it seems to stem from the influence of a bad or disinterested parent.

For example, in the 1880s, we find members of the Thurstance, Wallace and Rotchell families cropping up over and over again in reports of court proceedings at Penkridge, alongside one-man-crime-wave Isaac Pearson! Their actions - mostly drunkenness, fighting and using foul language - must have been a considerable nuisance to villagers and tiresome for those officers who had to deal with them time and time again.

One evening in the autumn of 1886, the Star Inn and the George & Fox were each the scene of spectacular brawls between two groups of men, one of whom was Henry Thurstance. It was during the Penkridge Wakes and gardener William Bennett and his friends were drinking at the Star Inn when a group of men entered the pub and declared that they could dance or fight (!) better than any man in the place. Unsurprisingly, a fight soon broke out but before long order was restored and both groups left the premises. A little while later, at around nine o'clock, they met again, this time at the George & Fox, and a mass punch-up ensued.

One of the men involved, John Williams a Chadsmoor miner, found himself in court at the Cannock Petty Sessions, charged with a serious assault on Bennett. During the second altercation, Bennett was struck on the head by a heavy jug, allegedly thrown by Williams. He suffered two severe cuts to his brow and temple and his skull was fractured.

Thurstance and two other local labourers, William Hodgkiss and Thomas Jackson, and a lad named Thomas Plant, all swore that Williams had thrown the jug and that he could be easily identified because of the unusual light-coloured suit he was wearing.

Several people who were in the George & Fox, and not associates of Williams, testified that it was not Williams who had thrown the jug although they couldn't say who had. Williams' defence was essentially mistaken identity, as his brother Thomas, who was also there, was dressed in a very similar outfit. Thomas Williams confessed that he was involved in the fight but said he saw a man in a dark jacket throw the offending vessel. The bench decided that despite the contradictory evidence, the matter should proceed to trial at the next Assizes.

William Thurstance, the above mentioned Henry's brother, got more than he bargained for when he crossed swords with Carrie (Keziah) Wallace earlier that same year. Mrs Wallace, wife of John Wallace mentioned elsewhere, went to find out what he had been doing to her daughter, who had complained about him. It wasn't until Mrs Wallace was returning home that Thurstance plucked up the courage to leave his house and confront her. At the Petty Sessions, Mrs Wallace alleged that Thurstance had overtaken her, then turned around and struck her in the mouth.

The only witness, draper's assistant John Thacker, said he heard Mrs Wallace calling Thurstance to "come and have it out" but he could not say whether Thurstance had struck the woman. The bench dismissed the case but Thurstance had already paid in part for whatever he had done: at the end of the confrontation Wallace had knocked him down! Thurstance was an agricultural labourer living on Mill Street, but a family of that name, including an 11 year old William, actually lived next door to the Wallaces on Market Street in the early years of that decade.

In summer 1894, the Wallaces and Thurstances were feuding once more. This time Edward Thurstance, a quarryman, his wife Emily and daughters Annie (17) and Emily (15) were charged with assaulting Annie (21) and Sarah Jane Wallace (19). The complainants alleged they were passing the Thurstances' house when Annie shouted some insult at them and then ran at the pair, knocking Sarah Wallace over. Mrs Thurstance then called out "pull the ***** cat into the house and I'll kill her with the poker" at which point the Wallaces were dragged inside and set upon by the whole family!

Eventually the young women managed to escape, but without their hats, and rushed home to tell their parents. Mr and Mrs Wallace then went to the Thurstances' house to demand the return of their daughters property only to find that the hats had been completely torn to pieces.

The Thurstance sisters told a contradictory story and had issued cross-summonses, alleging that it was the Wallace sisters who were the aggressors and that they had also threatened to kill Mrs Thurstance! Fortunately the event was witnessed by Edward Rutter, a mason of Stone Cross, who saw Sarah Wallace strike the first blow then force entry to the Thurstances' house. When he saw the lot engaged in a scrimmage on the floor of the property he walked off and left them to it, no doubt shaking his head!

Lord Hatherton, describing the entire episode as "most disgraceful", fined Sarah Wallace twenty shillings plus another sixteen in costs, or twenty one days with hard labour in default. Upon payment of costs by each party, he dismissed the other cases.

In 1902, Harry Thurstance and his friend Joseph Handley were charged with obstructing the footpath on the corner of Market Street. Constable Flavell had watched the pair for about 10 minutes, while they stood drinking, forcing other pedestrians to step into the road. The court however had little choice but to dismiss the case due to lack of corroboration.

In February of that year, William Thurstance was fined forty shillings plus costs for being drunk and disorderly and assaulting the police - it had taken both Sergeant Campbell and Constable Knight to literally carry him, kicking and screaming, to the police station. Seven months later, Fanny Thurstance and several friends were before the Bench accused of using bad language while drinking at Charles Bott's house. They were all fined around ten shillings including costs. Miss Thurstance, who had railed against the police, accusing them of lying, was recalled and handed a further fine of 1s 6d

Two weeks later William was back in court on another charge of drunkenness, this time for trying to enter the White Hart when already drunk. When he refused to leave, it became necessary to forcibly eject him. The matter didn't end there though; the landlord of the Crown Inn - where Thurstance had been drinking before visiting the White Hart - was charged with permitting drunkenness and Thurstance's sisters and father were charged with obstructing the police and incitement to resist arrest! His father, John Thurstance was also charged with using obscene language at the time of the incident. All cases were proven and typical fines imposed.

Come summer it was the turn of John Thurstance to appear before the magistrate. He was charged with using "the most disgusting" bad language in his house and doing it so loudly that the neighbours complained. Thurstance was the worse for drink when he arrived at court and declared that "if a man could not speak as he liked in his own house, he ought not to live", to which Mr Thorneycroft replied: "And a man who uses language as you have done ought not to live". He said it was no use fining the defendant lightly - he would pay one pound plus costs or serve 14 days in gaol. Thurstance left the court shouting "I won't pay it, I'll do it like a man. I have paid enough here".

A few weeks later, John and William Wallace, scrap dealers of Stone Cross, were each fined 1s plus 8s 6d in costs for using bad language... in their own house! P.C. Flavell provided the evidence - one can only assume that he stood by an open window or door to note down their outburst.

Isaac Pearson, a general labourer and army reservist, lived with his mother Jane at 46 Town End (on Cannock Road). Late in May 1894 he appeared at the Police Court, charged with drunkenness and assaulting a police officer. Pearson was no stranger to the courtroom, having been previously fined for being drunk and disorderly on the Cannock Road. This time around, twenty-six-year-old Pearson brought a counter-summons against the arresting officer, Constable Hollins.

According to P.C. Hollins, he went to Mrs Pearson's house, following reports that her son was drunk and smashing up crockery, and found a large crowd of people gathered outside. Inside, the house was in general disorder and in the kitchen he found Pearson, drunk and in a very belligerent mood. When the constable asked him to quieten down and behave, Pearson pulled off his waistcoat and braces, ran at Hollins and struck him in the eye. Following a brief struggle Pearson was subdued, handcuffed and carted off to the station.

Pearson's story was rather different; he claimed that Hollins came into the house, threw him on the floor, struck him in the face, held him by the throat and knelt on his chest! Council for the defence argued that Hollins had exceeded his duty and that in the course of the arrest he had kicked Pearson and knocked out one of his teeth.

A large number of witnesses were brought before the Bench for both parties but despite two witnesses claiming to have seen blood on Pearson's face, Mr Perry, the magistrate, dismissed the case against Hollins saying that as an officer with five years service, he wouldn't be so foolish as to assault a man in such a manner. Pearson was fined ten shillings plus costs. Unlike the court, Mrs Pearson must have been prepared to overlook the episode as the pair were still living in the same house at the turn of the century.

In March of the following year Pearson was back in court, this time as a witness, because of his involvement in two related cases. The first concerned the conduct of farmer Joseph Holt and the second an assault by Albert Thurstance at the same incident.

Holt was charged with being drunk and disorderly on 2nd February. According to Sergeant Titterton, Holt's son was driving a cart with Holt senior sat beside him in a very drunken state and using bad language. When they reached the White Hart, Holt got down from the cart and was told by the officer to mind his language. While Titterton examined their cart-horse, which was sweating and trembling badly because it was lame, Holt went into the inn's yard, mounted another horse and tried to ride off. Sergeant Titterton and Constable Foxall managed to grab the second horse and Holt was persuaded to dismount. Shortly afterwards Holt remounted the horse but once again the officers managed stop him, this time shutting the door to the yard as well.

Eventually, Holt was allowed to continue on his journey home provided that he moderated his language and his son kept the reins. Constable Foxall told the court that Holt was very obstinate and caused a lot of trouble before he finally calmed down and was allowed to leave. Holt called John Simcox, a wagoner, and Albert Thurstance as witnesses, both of whom were in the yard of the White Hart at the time. Both told the court that Holt was sober and that the officers had acted unreasonably. The Bench did not agree and handed Holt a small fine plus costs or fourteen days in default.

Immediately after this case, Thurstance was charged with assaulting Constable Foxall. The officer told the court that while he was helping restrain the horse that Holt was trying to ride away, Thurstance charged at him, grabbed him by the throat and pushed him away. Foxall said that Thurstance was "acting like a madman", pushing and pulling him, trying to dislodge his grip on the horse.

Thurstance claimed that the constable's statement was a lie and called Isaac Pearson as a witness. Pearson said he didn't see Thurstance anywhere near the horse, although it was very dark in the yard at the time. Simcox was also called and said he didn't see Thurstance strike the officer or put his hand on the bridle. Once again, the court was inclined to believe the police version of events and Thurstance was fined 20s plus 11s costs or a month in default.

Before these two cases were heard, Holt was also charged with 'negligent driving' on an earlier date. On that occasion the same officers were on duty in Clay Street when they heard a horse and cart coming slowly towards them from the direction of Stafford. In due course the vehicle turned around and continued in the direction from whence it had come. Suspecting something amiss, Foxall ran to the cart and stopped it as it seemed to have no driver. However, when he climbed up onto the vehicle he found Holt lying on his back in the cart, fast asleep, with the reins between his legs!

When woken up, Holt appeared to be sober and when asked what he meant by letting the mare wander as it pleased he simply said, "It is all right"! Sixteen shillings was the total penalty imposed.

Six months later Isaac Pearson was in trouble again, this time charged under the London and North Western Railway's bye-laws with "having interfered with the comfort of passengers" and with having assaulted three men: Joseph Smith, Stephen Redfern and Joseph Shackleford.

The victims were all members of a Walsall rambling club and, after a good day's walk and dining in the village, were waiting to take a train home at about 10pm. Pearson, who was once again 'under the influence', became annoyed at their good humour and singing, and approached them brandishing a stick. He hit Shackleford three times across the chest and Smith upon the head, at which Smith jumped onto the track out of Pearson's reach.

Hearing the commotion, the station master came out of his office and ushered Pearson away, telling him not to harass the passengers. Pearson wasn't finished yet though, as he now charged at Redfern and struck him. Redfern managed to return a punch before the pair fell to the ground then rolled onto the metals, seriously damaging the muscles in Redfern's left arm. Pearson struggled to his feet and began to kick Redfern, cutting him above the eye. A number of the ramblers tried to pull Pearson off but it was only when a train was approaching that the stationmaster finally managed to drag him away.

At the Police Court, Lord Hatherton imposed a 20 shilling fine for interfering with passengers' comfort, six weeks imprisonment for the assault on Smith, three months for his "cowardly and unmanly assault" on Redfern and fourteen days for the assault on Shackleford.

Whereas the Thurstances and Wallaces seemed to be most active in the final decade of the nineteenth century, the name Rotchell begins to appear in cases at the end of the first decade of the new century, although one Thomas Rotchell, doubtless an ancestor, was a victim of crime in the 1830s - James and Thomas Bates were each imprisoned for two months with hard labour for stealing clothing from him.

Thomas Hollingshead, a miner of the Flax Ovens, was charged with using obscene language on 28th December 1909 - he had six previous convictions for the same offence. In court Hollingshead said that after his last hearing, Constable Collins told him he would watch his house day and night and "have him again". Lord Hatherton's riposte being: "Very properly, he has got you again". Holingshead created an outburst of laughter when he accused Collins of walking up the road with his arm around a young woman named Matilda Rotchell, something that the officer categorically denied and which was born out when the woman in question was called before them. Imposing a fine of one pound plus costs or fourteen days detention, his Lordship told Hollingshead that the heavy fine was intended to stop "this disgusting language".

In early 1910, a thirty-year-old collier named John Rotchell who lived at the Goods Station, was brought before the Police Court for assaulting a little boy. Rotchell and his younger brother were walking along Market Street when the younger sibling threw a stone that hit the back of Charles Bickley. As they walked on, the brothers eventually caught up with Bickley and the elder one hit him, knocking him down. Following the attack, witness Fanny Neville said that young Bickley had a lump on his head the size of a teacup!

Rotchell claimed that Bickley had been knocking his brother about and that was why he had given him "a clout". Lord Hatherton said that a great big man hitting a small boy deserved a severe fine and imposed ten shillings plus thirteen in costs. It is hard to believe that Charles Bickley was just four years old.

Just as the women of Penkridge were the equal of men when it came to consuming alcohol, they also denied men the monopoly on fighting and threatening behaviour.

A year or so into the Great War, Annie Tomlinson of Mill Street, whose husband was an artilleryman serving on the front lines, issued a summons against Mary Jane Rotchell, Matilda Lloyd and Mary Hartwell for threatening behaviour, and the three ladies in question each issued a cross-summons against Tomlinson for the same reason.

The women were neighbours, and Mrs Tomlinson alleged that her life had been a misery because the other three women were continuously overlooking her yard and abusing her. Mrs Tomlinson said she also feared for her life as they had made numerous threats, saying they would "do her down" if they caught hold of her.

The defendants denied making any threats, Rotchell saying that Tomlinson called her "a dirty old cat" and had also threatened to "ring her neck out". Hartwell said Tomlinson had threatened to thrash her son and to "scald her eyes out"! The defendants were bound over to keep the peace for 12 months and the cross-summonses were dismissed.

In a separate but probably related case heard on the same day, Fanny Ellsmore was charged with assaulting Sarah Rodwell with a broom. Rodwell had given evidence in the earlier hearing, and as might be expected, a cross-summons was also issued in this case. This time, both parties were bound over for twelve months.

Referring to the drink that seems to have played a part in both cases, Lord Hatherton remarked that there was either too much money flying around between these parties or, if there was not too much, they did not know how to spend it properly.

As the old saying goes, you can choose your friends but you can't choose your family and sometimes family members get under each other's skin to such an extent that they come to blows. One such case concerned another two Rodwell family members - Elizabeth and her sister Mary Manford, one living at Market Square and the other at Fox Holes. Both were in their early thirties at the time of this incident and both were married to chimney sweeps (perhaps this had something to do with their falling out?).

At about 8pm in late April 1870, Mary stepped out of her house on the way to the village centre, when she met her sister and brother-in-law, Charles Rodwell. Almost immediately, Mrs Rodwell hit Mrs Manford and the pair began to fight, with Rodwell being egged-on by her husband! When Mr Manford heard his wife's cries he ran out of their house to help, but he was attacked by Mr Rodwell, who knocked him down.

Both Rodwell's were found guilty of assault, Mr Rodwell being fined over £1 in total with a month in default and his wife 15s including costs or 14 days detention. No reason for the attack was reported.

Some families of course are very close, and a bizarre prosecution reported in February 1899 shows, quite literally, how close one particular family was. Enoch Bott of Clay Street was prosecuted for "permitting a nuisance to exist on his premises". Specifically, it was a case of overcrowding; Bott, his wife, his adult daughter and 21-year-old grandson were all sleeping in the same small room.

According to the council sanitary inspector, the room offered a total of 980 cubic feet of air, when the rules required 300 cubic feet per person. Assuming that the room was of average height it would have a floor area of perhaps 10 by 12 feet, which doesn't seem excessively small considering the cramped and insanitary conditions that some people lived in at that time.

Exactly how the health inspector knew that they were sleeping in the same room in the first place is a mystery, but a follow-up visit by Sergeant Campbell about 10 days later found all four still sharing the same room. We will have to imagine the exact circumstances of the policeman's visit as it is not recorded!

Mr Bott was landed with over 14 shillings in costs and an abatement order. Having done his calculations, he informed the court that his daughter now slept at a neighbour's house most of the time. At the time of the 1901 census, his wife and daughter were still at the address but Mr Bott was elsewhere.

Abandoned and Abused

For those determined to do so, abandoning spouse and family must have been considerably easier in the past, particularly at those times when labour was in demand, making it easy to 'up-sticks' and find employment elsewhere. Before the advent of a nationwide police force and the sort of record-keeping that we now take for granted, men especially, could slip away, leaving their cares and responsibilities behind them.

Those abandoned might have been able to obtain a court order against the absconder or, if in dire financial circumstances, seek the help of the 'overseers of the poor', the Board of Guardians. In either case a reward might be offered for information leading to the whereabouts of the deserter.

One of the earliest records regarding a Penkridge resident is that relating to Thomas Bird, in 1802, who was apprehended and hauled before the court at Stafford to face the music. Bird was another of those persistent offenders; in the following three years he appeared at the same court on charges of squatting, breach of the peace and assault!

In 1805, John Finney of the village was tried for abandoning his family and in 1812 James Costing was imprisoned for a month for deserting his. James Whiston appeared at Stafford in both 1814 and 1815 on the same charge and he was sent back to Penkridge to serve his sentence.

William Adams, a Penkridge railway worker, deserted his wife and children in 1839, forcing them to enter the Workhouse, which had recently been relocated to Brewood. Adams had worked on the construction of the Grand Junction Railway in the preceding years and was known to his workmates as 'Little Will', on account of his short stature. In their advertisement offering a £3 reward for his apprehension, the Guardians described him as 28 years old, around five foot six with light hair, blue eyes and a fresh complexion. He had been punished for abandoning his family on a previous occasion, as well as spending time in prison for assaulting a policeman.

Penkridge Board of Guardians summoned six brothers to court in January 1868. Despite all of them being in employment, they refused to provide financial support for their mother, Ann Taylor, who was in her seventies. She had a further four sons but every one of the ten tried to pass responsibility to the other.

Ann had lived for a time with her son William but he had treated her so badly, that she would not live with him any longer and she ended up being supported by 'out-door relief' from the Union. Describing their conduct as shameful, the Bench adjourned the case to determine the contributions that each of her sons should make.

In 1899, Luke Blent, a groom, was brought to court because he hadn't paid any maintenance to his wife. The hearing was adjourned in order to verify his claim that he had been ill. Two years later, Albert Faulkner was jailed for a month for failing to pay a maintenance order of ten shillings per week to his wife Harriet. Mrs Faulkner had taken out a warrant about nine months earlier, at which time he was already over a year in arrears. On the day he was sent down, the total owed stood at over £47.

Mrs Faulkner lived on Clay Street with her eighteen-year-old daughter and neither of them were employed. Mrs Faulkner did have some income however, as she had two middle-aged boarders at the time of the case.

In 1913, a Mrs Robinson of Mickleover, Derbyshire was summoned by the Police Court on behalf of the Cannock Board of Guardians. Her husband was an inmate and she should have been contributing six shillings a week towards his upkeep, but after three months she had not made a single payment. She could not claim her failure to pay was as a result of hardship - she owned property worth over £10,400, a very substantial sum in those days and equating to about £1 million today! The court issued an order for payment with costs.

For those trapped in a relationship with a controlling or psychotic partner or parent, where domestic violence was a factor, things must have been very grim indeed, especially in circumstances where money and the means to escape were non-existent.

Similarly, in an era when child labour and corporal punishment were the norm, neglected children would have had little hope unless they had a caring neighbour, aunt or grandmother.

Samuel Betts, a labourer, was in Drayton Lane, which at that time was bordered by a number of houses, when he saw wagoner John Wedge and his wife Frances. Suddenly Wedge grabbed his wife by the head and thrust her neck down on a fence. When she collapsed in a heap, Wedge then proceeded to kick her.

Despite Betts and another person witnessing the attack, Mrs Wedge, a young woman who was deaf and dumb, refused to press charges against her husband. It was therefore left to the police to lay the information before the court in May 1878. Mrs Wedge was questioned in writing, something that she was able to do very adeptly through extensive practice, but refused to make a statement against her husband.

Mr Perry, for the Bench, said that it was one of the most disgraceful and brutal cases that had ever been brought before them and that John Wedge was one of the most abominable wretches he had ever had to deal with. He said that he would have sent Wedge down for the maximum period except for the hardship that it would inflict upon his poor wife.

As it was, Wedge was sentenced to three months with hard labour and a public subscription to support his wife during his incarceration was begun there and then. However, Mrs Wedge was described as "greatly agitated" at the outcome of the trial, no doubt fearful that she would ultimately pay the price.

Fear of reprisal was most likely the reason that Gertrude Handley failed to appear at the magistrate's court in 1915, after bringing a charge of assault against her husband Joseph, a collier. The previous year Mrs Handley had appeared before the court for using "language bad enough for a man but disgraceful for a woman". She was let off, upon payment of costs, as the Bench decided that her undignified outburst was as a result of provocation, having been struck in the mouth by her husband! The pair, who were both around forty years old, had been married for over twenty years and lived at Flax Ovens off Goods Station Lane with their seven children.

Sarah Ann Hodgkiss and her mother, Sarah Hodgkiss, were each fined five shillings plus costs for ill-treating a young relative, Richard Cooksey, in early 1899. The older woman, his grandmother, had kicked him and his aunt had thrown a knife at him. The lad was sent to the Cannock workhouse where he would almost certainly have received kinder treatment.

Elizabeth Leach of Mill Street was cautioned at the Petty Sessions for mistreating her son John, aged 13. It was the second time Leach had appeared before the magistrate in a month – on the first occasion she was fined sixpence for using bad language whilst at her brother's house in Market Street.

John told the hearing that his mother had asked him to wash the dishes but he didn't want to because he was too tired – hardly surprising given that he'd had nothing to eat that day, other than something taken from a neighbour's pig bucket. He went off to bed but shortly his mother got him up and pushed him to the kitchen to carry out the chore.

Sergeant Campbell said that when he visited the house, the child's room was dirty and cold and the boy had bruises on his face like fingermarks. He said that the boy's mother was often drunk and he had noticed on several occasions that the child wasn't well looked after.

Their neighbour, Emma Jones, said she had seen Leach hit John in the stomach with a mop. Mrs Jones had given him food in the past and had even seen him scraping up crumbs that she had put out for the birds because he was so hungry.

By the following year, young John had escaped from his mother's 'care' and was working as a servant at Plashes Farm, Acton Trussell - a hard life, but one where he would at least have been regularly fed. By the time he was sixteen he was married with a son, also named John, and was living at The Marsh.

In 1895, forty-one year old Catherine Fletcher was brought to court by the NSPCC for neglecting her four children, aged between 5 and 13. The court heard that her husband had recently left because of her drunken habits and although the family had been granted a place at the workhouse, she did not take up the offer, presumably because she would not be allowed to drink if admitted.

Instead she remained at home and gradually pawned every available possession to support her addiction, to the utter neglect of her children. They all had bruises or wounds as a result of being hit, some of which had become badly infected. Their clothes were ragged and infested with lice, the house was devoid of food and warmth and an oak table was the only piece of furniture she still possessed.

A neighbour, Eliza Martin, told the magistrate that Fletcher often returned home drunk, and regularly left her children unattended for many hours at a time. Recently the eldest child had come to her house in tears, saying that his mother had bitten his hand; on examination the flesh had been bitten right through to the bone. When confronted by Mrs Martin, Fletcher threatened to bite the other children too!

As is often the case with such people, the woman had a string of previous convictions. On this occasion she was handed a one month custodial sentence with hard labour. In reply to the pronouncement she could say nothing more than "Very well. Thank you."

In the same year, John Terry and Maria Cottrell were fined ten shillings apiece for neglecting their five children. Once again, children and house were in a filthy condition and the premises were almost completely devoid of furniture.

In 1901, single mother Annie Bradbury of The Marsh, was fined ten shillings for failing to send her daughter Ethel to school. Childcare was obviously an issue for the woman but within three years she had found a husband in haulier Walter Thomas and, presumably, an easier life.

In 1911, the village was awash with rumour that the death of 11-year-old Vivian William Barnacle was the result of an assault by his father, William, a bricklayer of Market Place. The lad had been admitted to Stafford Infirmary after becoming delirious and developing a huge swelling around one eye. Because the rumours had already come to the attention of the police and the NSPCC, an inquest was considered necessary.

It was unfortunate that on the night that the lad became seriously ill, his father was uncharacteristically the worse for drink and his mother was away for the day. When alerted to the condition of the boy by his daughter, Mr Barnacle and a neighbour tried various simple remedies, believing that he had either been stung, or was suffering from neuralgia or toothache. In the morning, Mr Barnacle was so hung-over that he sent his son to the shops, despite the child being so poorly. Turning up in the village with a swollen eye and in an insensible state no doubt gave rise to the gossip that he had been thumped by his father.

When Louisa Barnacle came home she summoned the doctor, who immediately had the boy sent to the Infirmary. Over the next few days, surgeons took steps to relieve the enormous swelling around his bulging eye but despite their efforts, his temperature rose and his condition gradually worsened until he died.

The inquest heard from surgeon Dr Cridland who had operated on the lad and carried out the post-mortem. He was able to categorically state that meningitis was the cause of death, the swelling around the eye being caused by necrosis of one of the orbital bones which had become soft and diseased. In his summing up, the Deputy Coroner said the hoped that the verdict of 'death by natural causes' would scotch the rumours once and for all. He said that they were "a very cruel and hard thing upon the parents" who were clearly devoted to their son. When a juror stated that no-one was against that suggestion, he was greeted with cries of "hear, hear".

Coroner Mr W. Morgan held an inquest on six-month-old Louis Roberts at the Boat Inn, in January 1887. He said his principal reason for holding the inquest, was so that it would serve as a warning to parents.

After being fed a mixture of chewed bread and sausage, the infant turned black in his mother's arms and died as a result of suffocation. Local surgeon Frederick Boldero, who lived at the Ivy House, told those present that it was not uncommon for the labouring classes to feed their babies totally inappropriate food, believing that as long as they chewed it up first, it would be safe for even the smallest babies to eat. “We give it the same as we have", was a comment he had heard time and again.

Just before the Great War, a case came before Lord Hatherton which he described as the worst case of depravity he had ever seen. It concerned Thomas and Minnie Luker of Biddle Bank, Boscomoor and the neglect of their children. An inspection by the NSPCC, which had three decades of experience in these matters by this time, found the Luker's house to be in a filthy and disgusting condition, and their children to be badly clothed and malnourished.

Furthermore, fourteen year old Ruby Farnell, Mrs Luker's illegitimate child, was deemed to be at risk of prostitution. When interview by the police, the girl said that she had been with two men and when questioned about this, her mother said she knew what was going on but was afraid to mention it to her husband.

The couple were each jailed for three months and Mrs Luker was bound over for a further twelve in view of the abject supervision of her daughter. Ruby had a poor start in life, being born in the Union workhouse, but within a decade of this episode, she had at least found a husband and settled down away from her parents.

Violence and Offences Against the Person

In May 1852, local policeman Reuben Billet was patrolling near the Boat Inn when Thomas Dobson, a large powerful man, leapt over a garden wall, ran at the officer and tried to stab him with a sharpened iron poker. Fortunately for Billet, his greatcoat and uniform prevented the point from penetrating his body and gave him chance to deal with a second thrust from Dobson, knocking the weapon from the attacker's hand. A struggle ensued but Billet eventually managed to gain the upper hand and kept Dobson pinned down until help arrived.

Dobson was carted-off to the lock-up and appeared before the magistrate two days later. In court it emerged that a little while before the assault, Constable Billet had ejected Dobson from the Boat Inn for being abusive towards the landlady. Although Dobson was almost certainly under the influence of drink when he attacked the constable, such a serious offence merited a severe penalty: he was fined £10, but this amount being beyond his means, he was committed to the house of correction for two months instead. It seems likely that the Thomas Dobson referred to was a tailor who lived on Cannock Street, in the vicinity of the Boat Inn, with his wife and two children.

Thomas Bancele and Henry Crane, two labourers on Coppice Farm had a disagreement which led to Bancele being charged with assault. He had approached the other man and asked him to go in to the village but when Crane refused Bancele knocked him down and proceeded to kick him. The violent outburst cost the aggressor a total of eleven shillings including costs.

It was common in the past for certain people to have more than one occupation, for example there were many farmers and blacksmiths who also worked as publicans or wheelwrights, or publicans who were also butchers. Walter Steel (36) of Clay Street had an unusual combination of occupations - he was a hairdresser, chiropodist and professional entertainer! In the summer of 1900, he was working in this latter capacity at a village sports event, in a field on the Wolverhampton Road, when he was attacked by Edward Brookes (23), the previously mentioned postman who lived with his parents on Mill Street.

Steel had been sending up balloons, probably 'Chinese lanterns', powered by spirit-soaked wadding, when Brookes came up to him. Steel greeted him with a friendly “hello”, but according to witnesses, Brookes grabbed a handful of wadding from an ascending lantern and threw it into the other man's face. Steel immediately fell to the ground with his face aflame. Newsagent Joseph Plant, who was assisting with the balloons, helped put out the flames and later conveyed Steel to a doctor.

In court, Plant said that during the attack, he heard Steel cry out that Brookes had done it, and this claim was backed up by a number of witnesses. One of these was eleven-year-old Leonard Parsons of Clay Street. He said Brookes was angry because he thought he had won the earlier obstacle race but Steel, who had been acting as referee, had placed him second.

Brookes refuted this version of events, saying that he was helping launch the balloons when Steel threw some spirit in *his* face and said "how do you like that?". Another postman, John Davis, backed-up Brookes' account, as did two other witnesses, William Jones and John Wint.

Steel suffered light burns as a result of the confrontation and told the court that he was unable to work for over a week. Were it not for this, the contradictory statements would probably have resulted in dismissal of the case, but as it was, Brookes was committed for trial at the Quarter Sessions. Brookes was still living in the village some six months later, when the 1901 census was taken, so any sentence imposed upon him must have been quite light.

Before the end of the decade, Brookes was working as a hairdresser as well as a postman - perhaps having taken over

Steel's business, as Steel had either moved away or died. Brookes now found himself before the local magistrate once more, this time for failing to pay wages due to an employee.

He employed John William Matthews as a hairdresser's assistant at 10 shillings a week plus board, but had fired him because his hands shook so badly that it was putting-off customers. One man, who Matthews had begun to shave, decided he did not wish to risk seeing the matter through to the end and left the shop holding a handkerchief over his half-shaved face! Despite Mrs Brookes and others backing up Brookes' account, the Bench found that Matthews had not been paid the wages that were due to him.

Local tailor William Dent found himself arraigned at the Petty Sessions in November 1880 on a charge of assault. He was asleep at the Horse and Jockey when the landlord's son, Thomas Hodgetts, woke him up and asked him to leave. The indignant tailor was having none of it and lashed out the man who had disturbed his sleep. Unknown to Hodgetts, his father had given permission for Dent to stay there and Hodgetts senior was called before the court to confirm the fact. Nevertheless, Dent was still fined 11 shillings for his violent outburst.

Towards the end of 1861 the ‘Offences against the Person Act’ came into being and it remains a foundation of our legal system today. The Act set out various offences in detail including murder, manslaughter, rape and sexual assault, as well as more archaic sounding offences, such as furious driving, obstructing or assaulting a clergyman in his duties, and interfering with someone who is authorised to preserve a shipwrecked vessel!

As well as defining the various types of sexual offences, it set out penalties and the ages at which such crimes took effect; for example having carnal knowledge of a girl under 12, abduction of a girl under 16 or procuring a girl under 21. Homosexuality was defined as an 'unnatural act' and the act of 'buggery' carried a minimum sentence of ten years penal servitude.

With forensic science in its infancy, a fledgling police force (cities outside London were not required to have a police force until 1857) and the difficulty of proving identity and age, the odds were stacked against victims obtaining justice for many crimes of a sexual nature. This was especially the case when it involved the word of a child against that of an adult. There is no doubt that such crimes were as prevalent as they are today but, the likelihood of them coming to light being much smaller, far fewer were reported in the press.

When such offences were proven, they generally carried severe penalties; for example, a number of sexual offenders were sentenced at Stafford Assizes in 1883, including one John Parton, a 27-year-old fireman, who was sentenced to twenty years in prison for the rape of a 16-year-old girl near Gailey.

In the last summer of the nineteenth century, local shoemaker Pierce Donovan was committed for trial at the Assizes for sexually assaulting a 10 year old girl. Donovan, a sixty-year-old Irishman, had previously lived in Wolverhampton with his wife and daughter but moved to Penkridge some time before 1894 - the year in which his wife passed away.

The local court heard that on 15th August, Ann Hollinshead went into Mr Donovan's shop to ask if he needed any errands running. He said he did not but she alleged that he then grabbed her, took her into the adjoining house and committed the assault. She told her mother and aunt what had happened and she was then taken to

Dr Boldero, who examined her and found evidence of the attack. Donovan denied the offence and called Charles Cooper as a witness. Mr Cooper said that he was in the shop on the day in question and had not seen the child enter, although he had seen her sister. Due to the serious nature of the offence the matter was forwarded to a higher authority.

The precise outcome of his trial is not known, although if found guilty, Donovan cannot have been severely punished; just over a year later he was living and working back in Wolverhampton.

Chapter 5 – Fire, Theft & Fraud

Fire

By the end of the nineteenth century, fire-fighting, like policing and many other public services, was under the control of local government with many hundreds of local brigades offering an ever-improving service, with wider and more responsive coverage.

At the start of the Victorian era however, things were very different; most fire engines and firemen were funded by parish councils or insurance companies, with facilities in rural locations usually being extremely limited.

Given the primitive equipment available, firemen would do their best to save lives and contain the blaze, but there was often little choice but to allow a fire to burn itself out. Villagers would also come out to help fight fires during day or night, not just through a sense of community spirit, but because their livelihood might indirectly depend upon it. A fire at a mill, farm, smithy or other village industry could easily have a knock-on effect on a large segment of the local population.

At that time, in the days of mail and stage-coach, the turnpike roads through Penkridge and along Watling Street, were important transport arteries. Coach operators would use inns, spaced at about eight mile intervals, to change horses and collect or deliver mail and passengers. In 1829, the Spread Eagle at Gailey, run by Ann Hyde, was such a coaching inn and it served the 'Hero' coach on behalf of its Manchester owners. The stables were managed by Ann's son James, their business being to accommodate and feed the four coach-horses but they had no control over the animals themselves - that was the responsibility of the company's horse-keeper, Samuel Roe.

Roe had been sent to Gailey around the beginning of April and he and Hyde seemed to rub each other up the wrong way from the outset. After a few weeks, Hyde wrote to the Manchester firm, asking them to dismiss Roe and send a replacement. Shortly after this letter was sent, there was a fire at the cart-house adjoining the stables, and because of what had passed between the two men, Roe was singled out as a suspect and indicted on a charge of arson.

When the case came to court, witnesses were called on behalf of Mrs Hyde, the prosecutrix, and Samuel Roe. James Hyde said that the alarm was raised about one in the morning and rushing to the thatched cart-house, he found three of the rafters, part of the wooden wall and some straw alight. All four horses were by that time out of the stable, two of them already harnessed, and making off in the direction of Four Crosses pursued by Roe.

Joseph Sargeant told the court that he and John Stacey had been drinking with Roe at the Plough Inn earlier that evening. When Stacey told Roe that he had better go, as the horses would soon need to be dealt with, Roe told him "I'll not go 'til I like, James Hyde is not my master". He told the other two men about Hyde's letter and was alleged to have said "damn his eyes, I'll be revenged upon him".

After leaving the Plough at around 10pm, the three men headed toward the Spread Eagle and, according to Sargeant, all were a little "tipsy". Stacey, who lived nearby, went home. Roe told Sargeant he could sleep at the stables and after fetching a candle from the inn to light a lantern, the men bedded down for the night, with Sargeant sleeping atop a tub of corn. He was woken a little later by one of the horses pushing him off the tub, to find the place full of smoke. Sargeant called out in panic and Roe shouted back directions from the adjacent stable. Finally the men got themselves and the horses out, Roe saying that he would rather rescue his animals than go and raise the alarm.

Ann Glover, who had also been at the Plough Inn that evening, told the court that she overheard Roe saying to another man: "what a fire there'd be, and what work there'd be at the fire", that is, it would take a lot to put it out. The alleged recipient of these remarks, Robert May, was also called to give evidence but he flatly denied that Roe had said any such thing.

The judge told the jury that they must only convict if they considered that Roe had wilfully started the fire, not if he had simply been negligent in positioning his lamp. With this in mind, the jury returned a not-guilty verdict and Roe was acquitted.

In the centuries preceding this case there are many records of capital punishment being imposed for the crime of arson, even in cases where the damage was modest and no loss of life was involved; in the 1600s there are even records of children suffering this fate. A 16-year-old was hanged at Chelmsford in the same year as the Spread Eagle case, for setting fire to farm buildings, so the judge was certainly not exaggerating when he told Roe that he would have left him for execution if the evidence was incontrovertible.

Arson was suspected at Mr Baxter's corn mill at Whiston in 1792, and the culprit would certainly have been executed if found and proven guilty, given that the building, valued at one thousand pounds, was entirely consumed in the blaze.

Another stable fire happened at the King's Arms in the village, back in the summer of 1780. The landlord, a Mr Tomlinson, lost two stables and four horses after a candle which had supposedly been carefully placed, set fire to some hay.

Yet another local stable was engulfed by fire in 1836, this time the property belonging to Mr Kent of Drayton. Five horses were rescued although a wagoner was seriously burned - the fire was thought to have been started by the wagoner's lad not taking sufficient care when extinguishing a candle.

There was a fire in an out-building at Wolgarston Farm in 1865, supposedly caused by a spark from a boiler setting fire to some chaff. The whole of the 'boiling-house' and the roof of the adjacent cow shed were destroyed but twelve cows tied up inside the shed were rescued. Fortunately, farmer Henry Wood, had insurance in place to cover the losses which totalled some £40. As a mark of appreciation, Mr Wood paid for a substantial roast beef and plum pudding supper at the George & Fox, for the seventy plus people who helped put out the fire.

In 1849 an entire Penkridge family was devastated by fire, but suffocated rather than burned. John and Mary Cresswell had two sons, William aged 27 (described in the parlance of the day as 'an idiot' i.e. mentally impaired, although he had been employed in lock-making) and John aged 17.

When they retired to bed on the fateful evening, Mrs Cresswell made up a fire in the room in which the couple and William slept, while John slept in a separate room. It was usual for them to rely upon the heat of the kitchen fire to warm the house but as brickwork around the kitchen grate was being repaired, and it was the middle of winter, they had little choice but to have a fire in their bedroom.

The following afternoon, the man who had been working in the kitchen returned for his tools, but found no-one was up. He waited around for some time before putting up a ladder to peer through a bedroom window. The grim event being discovered, the workman forced entry through the window to render what assistance he could. Mother and youngest son were already dead and Mr Cresswell succumbed a day or two later. It seems that William was removed to Wolverhampton hospital but died soon after.

In 1902 Thomas Holt, a 34-year-old miner appeared at Stafford Assizes charged with burning down a hay stack at Penkridge. It was alleged that Holt set fire to the stack because he was hungry and bored. After starting the fire, he went immediately to the police station and handed himself in, no doubt hoping to be taken into custody where he would at least be fed basic rations.

The judge noted that there was a long string of convictions against Holt dating back over almost twenty years, including one for arson, for which he had been imprisoned. He said that the man had tried to live in a decent way since his last conviction and as a result he would deal leniently with him on this occasion - three years penal servitude was considered a light enough tariff.

In February 1853, the Penkridge fire engine, which belonged to the Birmingham Fire Office, was deployed to tackle a blaze at Huntington. The engine was under the control of Thomas Cope (who was the village plumber at that time) and Police Inspector Pike, who lived on Bell Lane. It was considered quite a feat that they attended the scene in just under an hour, although they failed to stop almost an entire rick of barley being consumed by the flames.

Incidentally, in that same month, a fellow named Luke Hale had a set to with Inspector Pike. Hale was brought before the magistrate accused of using threatening language to a police officer. The Inspector had apparently applied his skills of detection to a case of onion-theft at Otherton and one of Hale's relations was found to be the culprit.

A couple of years before the Huntington blaze, the engine, this time under the supervision of a Mr Mason, attended a fire at Saredon Hall. On that occasion it was to deal with a fire in a cowshed; the alarm was raised by two Irish labourers who slept in the shed but who promptly disappeared once the family had been alerted! Three cows were lost, but the owner's livestock was covered by fire insurance.

Mr Cope, the plumber, was still putting out fires in 1861. William Walker of Gailey Ley was so pleased with the local fire service that he took out an advertisement, thanking his friends and Mr Cope for putting out the fire at his premises, and congratulating his insurers, Birmingham Fire Office, for paying up promptly. No doubt the advert was encouraged, or perhaps even paid for, by the Fire Office to drum up more business in the area.

Captain Dukes and the Penkridge Fire Brigade spent a marathon

13 hours putting out a fire in a Dutch barn at Bednall in 1915. The contents of Mrs White's barn were lost but the fire was prevented from spreading to her house and other outbuildings at Bogmoor Farm.

A few months, later the Captain and his men were involved in another prolonged fire-fight, this time at Otherton. Sergeant Woolley was patrolling on his bicycle near Stretton just after midnight, when he noticed a glow in the sky in the direction of Penkridge. Cycling as fast as he could, he soon arrived at Mr Holt's farm where he found three hay ricks ablaze.

Woolley pedalled off with all speed to the village and within a few minutes of ringing the fire bell, Captain Dukes, his men and their favourite engine 'Charlotte' were on their way to the conflagration. When they arrived they found that the fire had spread, engulfing a threshing machine belonging to another farmer.

By 1.30am people from the village had begun to turn up and render whatever help they could, but the flames were not finally subdued until a little after midday. The damage was estimated at £500, equivalent to about £50,000 today.

Theft and Fraud

Back in 1795, a generation before the start of Victoria's reign, the wealthier inhabitants of Penkridge and the outlying villages formed a society to pursue and prosecute "all manner of felons and receivers of stolen goods". With Sir Edward Littleton at its head and John Tomlinson of the King's Arms as treasurer, this fledgling 'neighbourhood watch' group vowed to chase down anyone committing Grand or Petty Larceny:

"more especially, house-breakers, horse-stealers, sheep-stealers, fowl-stealers, ... against our person or properties, and the aiders, abettors or accessories of such offenders, and also the receivers of any goods, effects or property, that shall be stolen from any of us"

Their list of offences included illicit fishing, tearing down hedges, setting springles (traps) and so on. Toll-gate keepers were implored to keep note of the horses passing through their gates, especially at night, and rewards for information leading to prosecution were set from 10 shillings to 10 pounds depending upon the seriousness of the offence.

In the following year, 1796, 33-year old Daniel Heywood was transported for seven years for stealing five bushels (around 200 pounds in weight) of potatoes from John Tart. Whether or not the above mentioned group had any hand in his arrest is not known.

Sometimes even transportation was not deemed a sufficient penalty for theft; indeed, capital punishment was occasionally imposed for what today would be considered relatively minor crime - burglary, horse and cattle stealing and so forth.

For this reason, Matthew Hanley must have considered himself lucky when apprehended for stealing wheat in the following year - he was publicly whipped and imprisoned for a month, although he was further detained for having evaded arrest when discovered stealing flour at Penkridge Mill five years earlier.

There was an attempted break-in at the home of Mr Pearson of Preston Vale a couple of years after the formation of the society, but the burglars fled empty handed after trying to force open the window to a room in which someone was sleeping.

Two homeless men carried out a burglary at Modwena House, Penkridge a year later. They stole money, bread, cheese, butter, cocoa, sugar, scissors, knives and other items from the occupier, Francis Bewley, having gained entry by prising out two windows. They denied any involvement when first accused but some of the items were found in their possession when arrested on a similar charge... at Chester!

Jane Lunt, a 21 year old domestic servant, was imprisoned for two months with hard labour for stealing a variety of items from her employer at Great Wyrley in 1885. Caroline Kitson had dismissed the girl for dishonesty and when the police searched Lunt's Penkridge home they found clothing, furniture, three sovereigns and some silver forks and spoons belonging to Mrs Kitson. They also found two cups that had been stolen from J.B. Benton's Coffee Tavern on Mill Street - a further month with hard labour was added for this second offence.

Farmland beside the canal was always vulnerable to theft, especially by less scrupulous boatmen who wanted to supplement their meals for free. Whether it was crops, fruit, game or livestock, the temptation for many men (and sometimes their entire families) must have been just too great.

In 1864, boatman Thomas Bolton was up before Reverend Fell at the Petty Sessions, charged with stealing five turnips worth 3d. It was thought necessary to make an example of Bolton because £5 worth of turnips had been stolen from that field alone during the year. He was fined ten shillings plus costs or 21 days in prison in default – not having the money to pay, he would at least be fed legally every day for three weeks!

A field near the wharf at Gailey suffered severe pilfering in the autumn of 1866, when farmer Mr Hill lost almost an entire acre of turnips to boatmen. One of the thieves, Robert Little, was apprehended and brought before the court at Penkridge. As he couldn't afford the 10s plus costs either, he also served twenty one days imprisonment.

With merchandise constantly moving in and out, canal wharves were also a frequent target for the light-fingered. For example, Richard Hazel, a rag-and-bone man of Bog Green, Teddesley Hay, was sent to the house of correction for seven days in 1866 for stealing two pieces of larch, worth four shillings, from Thomas Stringer, the wharf-keeper at Penkridge.

Just after the start of the Great War, Thomas Lawton was fined 35s at the Police Court, for stealing coal from a wharf belonging to West Cannock Colliery. P.C. Dale spotted Lawton and another man, who seems to have escaped, helping themselves to the fuel at midnight.

Canal-side pubs also saw more than their fair share of petty crime. Catherine (Kate) Duffield, wife of a 'general dealer' of Pye Green, Hednesford had been to the Police Court at Penkridge on 1st November 1886 and then went to the Boat Inn. There she met Frances Bromwich, an itinerant hawker, and the pair got into conversation, with Duffield buying beer for the other woman. When they left the pub and stepped into the yard, Mrs Duffield felt Bromwich's hand enter her pocket. She thought nothing much of it at the time, but after setting off for home, noticed that she was missing five shillings and ninepence halfpenny. She immediately turned around and went in search of the other woman and having finally caught up with her, accused her of stealing the money.

Somehow, the tipsy pair ended up at the police station, where Constable Whitehouse searched the accused and found five shillings and ten-pence halfpenny – a penny more than the missing amount. Bromwich claimed that she had received one and a half shillings from a local tradesman and that the remainder was her own money. When the officer made enquiries, he found her statement to be correct.

Nevertheless, Duffield prosecuted and the matter was brought to the Petty Sessions at Cannock. In court, Bromwich claimed that the pair had got drunk together at the Boat and she categorically denied having taken the money. The Bench decided that as prosecutrix and accused were both drunk at the time, there was no clear case to answer and it was dismissed.

Enoch Downs was arrested while passing through the village in 1867 and charged with stealing a pair of stockings (i.e. socks, not women's hosiery). The garments belonged to Stafford Gaol, from where he had been released a few days earlier. The Deputy Governor of the prison declined to press charges, saying that his prison officers were to blame for allowing such a thing to happen. One can imagine that he made his views clear to his men in due course.

At the April 1869 Quarter Sessions, 24-year-old Betsy Ball was indicted for breaking into Penkridge Railway Station and stealing two pairs of trousers. She was arrested after pawning the clothes at Bilston, although she claimed she had got them from a man named Edward Lewis, who had since absconded. Whoever had broken in via a window on the night of 3rd March, had also stolen nine shillings and various small items. Ball was found guilty of receiving stolen goods and, having three previous convictions, was given a hefty six month jail term.

George Harvey, a "distressed looking person" of Wolverhampton admitted carrying out a number of thefts at Penkridge in late 1884. He stole several brushes from Maurice Day's coach-house and tools from the blacksmith's shop on Mr Keeling's farm at Congreve. He was also found to be responsible for a burglary at Brewood Grammar School (now the Middle School) a fortnight beforehand. The stolen property was recovered from a "common lodging house" in Wolverhampton and Harvey was committed for trial at the Quarter Sessions.

In August 1912, there was a burglary at St Michael's church and over four shillings from the offertory box and a pair of gold rimmed glasses were stolen (along with a list of hymns according to one report!). But it wasn't long before the culprit was discovered, as he handed himself in to the police at Shrewsbury.

Forty-seven-year-old Walter Chapman, of no fixed abode, was formerly a ship's cook. Due to the dock strike, he had been unable to find employment since being paid off at Middlesbrough. He freely admitted to taking the articles from the church and having spent the stolen money on food because he hadn't eaten for two whole days.

When returned to Penkridge to be charged, he said that he had given himself up because “I knew I would do something else and I didn't want to get into further trouble. When you cannot get food you have to do something”.

Schoolgirls Elsie Moorhouse (aged 13) and Alice Oldham (aged 12) wanted food too, but not any old food – they wanted sweets – and they stole them from three different shops in the village, along with a quantity of hair-pins and a vase! The older girl was the brains behind the operation, stepping carefully into each shop so as not to ring the doorbell and taking the nearest items from the counter. They were both found guilty of theft at the Police Court and were placed on probation for two years from June 1913, with their parents being bound over in the sum of £5 for each girl, as well as having to pay court costs.

Emma Healey was sentenced to a month in prison in 1883 for stealing a total of one shilling. She offered to take two sixpenny subscriptions to the Ancient Order of Forresters at Haughton on behalf of James Slinn of Mitton, but on both occasions she pocketed the money. Needless to say, Mr Slinn was rather surprised when informed that his subscriptions had not been paid and his wife Jane, who seems to have been a friend of Healey and tasked her with delivering the money, must have been mortified.

Being on the main road between two large towns, the shops and public houses of Penkridge must have been an attractive target for small-time fraudsters, who could conduct their 'business' then be on their way before their activities were uncovered, as these final few stories illustrate.

In 1858, Irishman James Allen was arrested for passing counterfeit coins at Mrs Wilk's grocery. Sergeant Oswell searched the man and found an old stocking containing 26 shillings and 3 florins in his jacket pocket, and one of each coin in his trouser pocket, all counterfeit. In addition he was found to be carrying over £1 in legal coin. The man was a hawker and had passed through the village with his basket of wares two weeks earlier, after which a substantial number of fraudulent coins had come to light.

George and Catherine Scarratt, a pair of vagrants, were charged with making a false statement to obtain poor relief. Mrs Scarratt went into the Police station to obtain tickets to the Workhouse, saying that she had no money and that her lame husband was waiting outside. However, as she left the station to rejoin her husband, Inspector Burgess overheard him say "I'll have half an ounce of 'bacca now you've got the tickets".

The pair went off to the White Hart where they ordered and paid for beer, little knowing that they had been followed by the Inspector. They were soon in court, where each was fined 5s plus costs or a week in prison in default.

Lord and Lady Hatherton made considerable efforts to relieve the hardship of the poor and needy in the winter of 1860, and this charitable behaviour seems to have attracted the attention of two "worthless vagabonds".

On 12th January 1861, John Wilden made a plea to Lady Hatherton for assistance. He claimed that he was a boatman, that his boat was frozen fast on the canal and that his pony had died from cold the night before. As a consequence, and having no money, he had no means to get back to his family who, he claimed, were in great want.

Taking pity on the man, her Ladyship provided him with dinner and a large bag of provisions, with a written order to obtain more from the village, along with a further order to the stationmaster to issue a ticket to Wolverhampton.

However, someone must have had suspicions about Wilden's story as he was very soon unmasked as a felon who had left Stafford Gaol that very morning after a three month sentence! He was very soon back inside, serving a further six weeks for his impudent fraud.

It seems almost inconceivable but Lady Hatherton was visited by another scoundrel just four days later. This fellow, John Barrett, an Irishman, called at Teddesley Hall claiming that he was starving. He was supplied with a generous quantity of bread and meat from the kitchens but left a few minutes later and was seen to throw the food away.

He called at the Hall again the following morning, but when questioned about the food he became abusive and said it was money he really wanted, not food. When Lord Hatherton was told of the matter, he ordered the man off the premises but Barrett steadfastly refused to leave. As might be expected, he was soon taken into custody and before long appeared at court, where he was sentenced to a month with hard labour for his roguish behaviour.

Reviewing all of these stories about the 'goings on' in Penkridge in times gone by, it is easy to find parallels with events in our own age. Despite ever increasing rules and regulations, improved policing and our more enlightened legal system, we still have accidents, criminality, mistreatment and misfortune caused by envy, anger, carelessness and plain stupidity. “There is nothing new under the sun” when it comes to human behaviour; it has influenced every event of the past and will surely continue to shape those still to come.

Sources

Chapter 1

One Over The Eight:
Staffordshire Advertiser 24th September 1831
Lichfield Mercury 1st February 1884
Lichfield Mercury 25th December 1885
Lichfield Mercury 7th May 1886
Lichfield Mercury 7th September 1888
Lichfield Mercury 24th August 1888
Lichfield Mercury 19 September 1890
Lichfield Mercury 8th November 1895
Lichfield Mercury 6th January 1899
Lichfield Mercury 6th April 1900
Lichfield Mercury 12th January 1900
Lichfield Mercury 30th May 1902
Lichfield Mercury 15th January 1909
Lichfield Mercury 18th September 1914
Lichfield Mercury 4th October 1901
Lichfield Mercury 30th May 1913
Lichfield Mercury 13th June 1913
Lichfield Mercury 22nd August 1913
Lichfield Mercury 15th May 1914
Shrewsbury Chronicle 29th April 1775

Meat, Fish and Poaching:
Lichfield Mercury 5th March 1880
Lichfield Mercury 9th November 1883
Lichfield Mercury 20th March 1903

Lichfield Mercury 17th November 1899
Lichfield Mercury 9th June 1882
Lichfield Mercury 7th November 1884
Staffordshire Advertiser 18th January 1868
Aris' Birmingham Gazette 6th December 1858
Staffordshire Advertiser 4th January 1851
Lichfield Mercury 27th October 1911

Miscellanea:
Staffordshire Gazette and County Standard 23rd January 1839
Worcester Journal 25th August 1877
Lichfield Mercury 27th June 1890
Lichfield Mercury 20th November 1896
Lichfield Mercury 11th July 1913
Lichfield Mercury 23rd February 1900

Chapter 2

Unexplained and Unfortunate Deaths:
Derby Mercury 11th January 1798
Staffordshire Advertiser 22nd April 1826
Staffordshire Advertiser 3rd March 1860
Staffordshire Advertiser 3rd December 1864
Staffordshire Advertiser 18th December 1852
Lichfield Mercury 7th November 1884
Birmingham Daily Post 13th July 1893
Lichfield Mercury 1st September 1911
Staffordshire Advertiser 9th June 1855

Cart and Carriage Accidents:
Staffordshire Advertiser 19th April 1823
Staffordshire Advertiser 19th September 1857
Staffordshire Advertiser 21st February 1863

Staffordshire Advertiser 6th February 1864
1881 census Piece number 2780 Folio 42 Page 33
Lichfield Mercury 27th June 1884
Staffordshire Advertiser 17th November 1866
Worcester Journal 15th February 1873
Preston Chronicle 15th July 1893
Lichfield Mercury 15th November 1901

Murder and Suicide:
Stamford Mercury 1st July 1791
Derby Mercury 15th May 1783
Staffordshire Sentinel and Commercial & General Advertiser 19th July 1856
Staffordshire Sentinel and Commercial & General Advertiser 26th July 1856
York Herald 12th July 1856
1851 census Piece 2018, Folio 121, Page 2
1861 census Piece number 389, Folio number 145, Page 67
Staffordshire Advertiser 6th June 1868
Manchester Courier and Lancashire General Advertiser 5th September 1896
Cheshire Observer 15th August 1896
Lichfield Mercury 11th September 1896
Staffordshire Advertiser 29th June 1799
Staffordshire Advertiser 17th January 1863
Birmingham Daily Gazette 11th January 1864
Gloucester Citizen 9th July 1887
Marriages Jun Qtr 1887 Cannock 6b 666
Staffordshire Advertiser 3rd December 1870

Chapter 3

On The Roads:
Staffordshire Advertiser 19th January 1833
Staffordshire Advertiser 26th December 1835
Lichfield Mercury 30th May 1913
Lichfield Mercury 15th May 1914
Staffordshire Advertiser 20th June 1863
Lichfield Mercury 24th January 1913
Lichfield Mercury 31st October 1913
Lichfield Mercury 22nd August 1913
Lichfield Mercury 18th June 1909
Lichfield Mercury 22nd August 1890
Lichfield Mercury 6th April 1900
Lichfield Mercury 23rd May 1884
1881 census, Piece number 2780 Folio 28 Page 5
Staffordshire Advertiser 21st April 1866
Lichfield Mercury 2nd November 1900
Lichfield Mercury 11th July 1913
Lichfield Mercury 9th May 1884
Lichfield Mercury 12th July 1912
Lichfield Mercury 29th July 1887

Rail Chaos:
Staffordshire Advertiser 11th February 1837
Berkshire Chronicle 13th January 1838
Western Gazette 12th October 1894
Staffordshire Advertiser 1st January 1853
Birmingham Daily Post 14th March 1861
Stamford Mercury 27th January 1865
Lichfield Mercury 4th April 1902
Staffordshire Advertiser 18th December 1869

Register of deaths Dec 1869 Stafford 6b 13
Leeds Mercury 26th September 1874
Lichfield Mercury 15th July 1881
Worcester Journal 20th August 1892

Water Woes:
Lichfield Mercury 9th March 1888
Staffordshire Advertiser 13th June 1846
Staffordshire Advertiser 6th October 1849
Liverpool Mercury 21st February 1870
Lichfield Mercury 21st August 1914
Staffordshire Advertiser 5th June 1802
Staffordshire Advertiser 26th November 1836
Lichfield Mercury 18th July 1902
Staffordshire Sentinel 24th June 1889
Staffordshire Advertiser 10th April 1869
Lichfield Mercury 18th July 1884

Chapter 4

Family Matters:
1881 census, Piece number 2780, Folio 27, Page 4 and Folio 41, Page 32
Lichfield Mercury 29th October 1886.
Lichfield Mercury 7th May 1886
Lichfield Mercury 7th September 1888
1891 census Piece number 2217 Folio 22 Page 6
Birmingham Daily Post 5th June 1894
Lichfield Mercury 8th June 1894
Lichfield Mercury 15th March 1895
Lichfield Mercury 11th October 1895
Lichfield Mercury 14th September 1894
1901 census, Piece number 2660 Folio 48 Page 11

Lichfield Mercury 5th September 1902
1901 census Piece number 2660 Folio 36 Page 21
Lichfield Mercury 5th September 1902
Lichfield Mercury 7th February 1902
Lichfield Mercury 21st February 1902
Lichfield Mercury 11th July 1902
Lichfield Mercury 19th September 1902
Lichfield Mercury 15th January 1909
Lichfield Mercury 28th January 1910
1911 census RG14PN16918 RG78PN1046 RD368 SD1 ED4 SN11
Lichfield Mercury 29th October 1915
Staffordshire Advertiser 7th May 1870
1871 census Piece number 2920 Folio 67 Page 2 and Folio 27 Page 2
Lichfield Mercury 24th February 1899

Abandoned and Abused:
Leicester Journal 27th December 1839
Staffordshire Advertiser 18th January 1868
Lichfield Mercury 19th May 1899
Lichfield Mercury 29th March 1901
1901 census, Piece number 2660, Folio 32, Page 14
Lichfield Mercury 5th September 1913
Lichfield Mercury 24th May 1878
Lichfield Mercury 10th February 1899
Lichfield Mercury 23rd February 1900
Lichfield Mercury 9th March 1900
Lichfield Mercury 6th September 1901
Walsall Advertiser 3rd August 1895
Lichfield Mercury 30th August 1895

Lichfield Mercury 15th September 1911
Births Sep 1899 Cannock 6b 536
1911 census RG14PN16919
Marriages Dec 1924 Cannock 6b 1086
Lichfield Mercury 21st January 1887
Lichfield Mercury 16th October 1914
Walsall Observer and South Staffordshire Chronicle 21st February 1914 (various errors)
Lichfield Mercury 11th June 1915

Violence and Offences Against the Person:
Staffordshire Advertiser 29th May 1852
1851 Census, Piece number 2016 Folio 66 Page 22
Lichfield Mercury 12th August 1887
1901 census, Piece number 2660 Folio 27 Page 3
Lichfield Mercury 7th September 1900
Lichfield Mercury 29th January 1909
RG14PN16917 RG78PN1046 RD368 SD1 ED3 SN114
Lichfield Mercury 12th November 1880
Lichfield Mercury 9th November 1883
Lichfield Mercury 25th August 1899
Deaths Jun 1894 Cannock 6b 255

Chapter 5

Fire:
Northampton Mercury 28th August 1780
Staffordshire Advertiser 15th August 1829
Staffordshire Advertiser 27th February 1836
Reading Mercury 20th February 1792
Staffordshire Advertiser 28th January 1865
Staffordshire Advertiser 4th February 1865
Staffordshire Advertiser 13th January 1849

Morning Post 15th January 1849
Deaths Mar 1849 Penkridge 17 96 and Wolverhampton 17 266
Tamworth Herald 26th July 1902
Staffordshire Advertiser 26th February 1853
Staffordshire Advertiser 28th December 1850
Staffordshire Advertiser 14th December 1861
Walsall Observer, and South Staffordshire Chronicle 23rd January 1915
Walsall Observer and South Staffordshire Chronicle 22nd May 1915

Theft and Fraud:
Stafford Criminal Records
Lichfield Mercury 31st July 1885
Staffordshire Advertiser 3rd December 1864
Staffordshire Advertiser 29th September 1866
Lichfield Mercury 12th November 1886
1891 census, Piece number 2219 Folio 128 Page 39
Staffordshire Advertiser 13th June 1795
Staffordshire Advertiser 12th August 1797
Staffordshire Advertiser 6th April 1799
Staffordshire Sentinel 14th August 1912
Lichfield Mercury 22th August 1913
Walsall Observer and South Staffordshire Chronicle 31st October 1914
Staffordshire Advertiser 27th October 1866
1871 census Piece 2920 Folio 53 Page 13
Staffordshire Advertiser 4th May 1867
Staffordshire Advertiser 10th April 1869
Lichfield Mercury 26th December 1884
Lichfield Mercury 23rd February 1900
Lichfield Mercury 13th June 1913

Lichfield Mercury 23rd August 1912
Lichfield Mercury 6th July 1883
Staffordshire Advertiser 1st May 1858
Staffordshire Advertiser 26th January 1861